Ordination of Women:
Interdenominational Perspectives

edited by

Cathy Thomson

and

Vic Pfitzner

ATF Press
Adelaide

Ordination of Women: Interdenominational Perspectives

Contents

Editorial

Discourse concerning the ordination of women to ministry in the Christian churches is over two hundred years old and spans the geographical regions of America, Europe, Africa, Asia and Australasia. Women have been present as ordained ministers in reformed churches since 1853. Yet the debate in the twenty-first century is still marked by a wide diversity of views. This ranges from stances that assert that it is patently clear that women are of equal calibre to men, that they are of equal dignity before God, and that they are equally susceptible to the calling of the Spirit of God who urges both women and men into diverse forms of service within the church. At the opposite end of the range are claims that women are clearly subordinate to men by biblical injunction. This view is also often supported by a suspicion of women as 'other', as anthropologically different from, or lesser than, men. In the middle are views which wish to support the equality in being, dignity and status of women and men, but which claim that God has apportioned to the sexes a different range of roles and ministries in life. In the church, it is claimed, this differentiation of roles becomes inviolable because of the establishment of an ecclesiological tradition which itself has gained immutability.

Predictably, arguments derived from tradition, from first-century practice and from biblical teaching are pressed into service by all shades of opinion in the debate. Equally, tools of exegesis such as literary and historical criticism are employed to form justifications across the whole gamut of views. Additionally, various interpretative postures in relation to biblical and historical material have resulted in the development of a range of hermeneutical frameworks within which this issue is postulated and appraised.

The papers included in this volume of Interface represent almost every nuance and shade of opinion that has been employed in the debate of women's ordination from its beginning. Contributors are drawn from a number of Christian denominations: Anglican, Baptist, Lutheran, Orthodox, Roman Catholic, and Uniting, and represent a number of different specialist areas within Australian theology.

Julia Pitman's paper sets the scene by providing a history of the ordination of women within Congregationalism in America, Britain and Australia. She tells the stories of inspired and inspiring women such as Antoinette Brown (ordained 1853 in America), Constance Todd (ordained 1917 in Britain), and Winifred Kiek (ordained 1927 in Australia). These three worked in situations where the issue of women's ordination was linked with the emancipation of women more generally, and in particular cases was directly associated with the women's suffrage movement. Pitman points out the considerable courage and perseverance of women scholars of the nineteenth and twentieth centuries who took on the challenge of their male counterparts by working in the field of historical and literary criticism to find theological justification for women's ordination. She also writes of the important role these early women played in offering pastoral care that for the first time was geared to the needs of female parishioners in the churches. Pitman points to the fact that Australia is exceptional in being slow to ordain women particularly because of the strength of non-conformist churches, and the relative weakness from the earliest days of the Church of England. Pitman finishes by suggesting that the 'double-burden' of home management and profess-sional career has made it difficult for women to pursue their ministries. She suggests that it is important that the role of advocating women's ordination be seen as the responsibility of the churches and not that of women alone.

Geoff Thompson articulates the Uniting Church's official stance with respect to women's ordination as this was first (if somewhat tentatively) conveyed in the 'Basis of Union', and given fuller and more developed expression in 'Why does the Uniting Church in Australia Ordain Women to the Ministry of the Word?' (WMOW). Here support for the ordination of women is viewed as a 'gospel imperative,' and is posited on three main principles: the interpretation of scripture, the priority of scripture over tradition, and the representative nature of the ordained ministry. With respect to scripture, Galatians 3:28 is emphasised, also what Thompson describes as the theological and chronological priority of male-female relations as practised by Jesus and taught by Paul. In claiming priority of scripture over Tradition, Thompson helpfully distinguishes between 'Tradition' which he claims is consonant with scripture, and 'traditions' which are varied in their expression. With respect to the representative nature of ordained ministry Thompson distinguishes a 'mimetic' from a 'referential' sense claiming the latter as the appropriate model for the Uniting Church, as this removes any sense that women are excluded from ordination because they cannot represent a male Christ. Thompson resists an impulse to return to origins to develop a claim for women's ordination, as he understands that all this provides is a picture of movement and sometimes discontinuity that coloured the life, ministries and relationships of the early church.

Our Lutheran writers, Peter Lockwood and John Kleinig provide exegetical exploration of two sets of biblical texts which often lead to contention in the ordination of women debate. Peter Lockwood identifies five pillars of argumentation based on readings of Genesis 2 and 3 which are often employed by Lutheran theologians to suggest that women are of a derivative status from men, that they are of a subordinate status and that that they have a greater susceptibility to evil than men. Lockwood wishes to critique the suggestion that these 'pillars' justify the preservation of ordination to men only. Lockwood supports the priority of scripture in any consideration of women's ordination, but he claims that the conclusions drawn from scripture are not always correct. Thus, claims that women have a derivative status with respect to men are critiqued on the basis of an exegetical model of Genesis which establishes a principle of 'becoming' of men and women which is mutual. Claims that women have a subordinated status are disputed with reference to the meaning of 'helper', a word applied to God in the Old Testament more frequently than it is applied to women. Lockwood is also at pains to point out the aetiological function of the punishments meted out to Adam and Eve. Rather than suggesting that Eve was more profoundly punished because of a greater susceptibility to sin, Lockwood suggests the text merely reflects and attempts to explain the observable fact that women experience pain in childbirth.

John Kleinig concentrates on the New Testament, and particularly on 1 Corinthians 14:33b–38 and I Timothy, 2: 11–15, which he suggests support the view of those opposed to the ordination of women. Kleinig claims that Paul is unequivocal in his exclusion of women from teaching in the church, and concludes therefore that they are prohibited from the apostolic ministry of the word. In referring to the passage from 1 Corinthians, Kleinig claims that Paul's prohibitions against women are applicable to all churches at all times; that they are firmly grounded in the whole of the Law of Moses; that they are authoritative as they are derived from a particular command of God to Paul; and that women who diverge from them are 'shameful'. From the Timothy passage Kleinig draws on the qualities of quietness and subordination as most appropriate for women, being clear that subordination is not to men in general but to Christ's word, and to the male teachers who teach the word. Kleinig finishes with a reaffirmation of his fervent belief that Christ has given to women neither the ministry of the word nor of the sacrament, and he warns that to hold such office(s) would be in direct violation of Christ's command.

Divergent views on the ordination of women in the Anglican Church are represented in the papers of Muriel Porter and Peter Bolt. In a lively paper, Porter acknowledges that the issue of the ordination of women is usually debated in the Anglican Church in an exceedingly cerebral manner, but suggests nevertheless that the origins of opposition to women's ordination lie in the fear men and women have of one another. Porter refers to the work of Bishop Max Thomas who was bishop of Wangaratta in 1976 and to the recent theological work of Dr Jane Shaw who visited Australia from the UK in 2004. Both have suggested that the only basis upon which a woman's suitability for ordination should be judged is whether or not God is calling her to that role. Porter suggests that in posing arguments in favour of women's ordination in negative terms of why women should *not be barred* from ordination, proponents have unwittingly colluded with opponents. If they had been positive from the beginning the church could hardly have failed to recognise in their midst the phenomenon of 'new wine in new wineskins'. Porter then unpacks the notion of male fearfulness of women, asserting that it goes deeper even than any psycho-spiritual malaise of the individual, as it emerges from the prevailing corporate prejudice that women are inferior to men. This, according to Porter, indicates the need within the Church for a 'comprehensive development of a theology of sexual equality'.

Peter Bolt describes himself as an Anglican Evangelical active in ministry in the diocese of Sydney. He is sensitive to any attempt to label groups of people or their actions as 'political' without grasping an understanding of the core belief systems underlying the politics. Within the life of Christian groups such core belief systems comprise love of God and of one's neighbour, and openness to repentance. In this paper, it is the processes which in the Anglican Church have led to the ordination of women that are to be repented of. Bolt desires to discredit liberalism which he characterises as a post-Enlightenment movement connected with the development of a free market, the dissolution of privilege, and a belief that the past was wrong and corrupt, and that present ideas are pure. Added to his resistance to these 'liberal' characteristics, Bolt also eschews the notion that progress is inevitable and that novelty must be a good thing in itself.

With respect to the church, Bolt asserts the necessity to repent of liberal excesses, particularly those, like the ordination of women, which he considers essentially opposed to God. He then makes a bid for the authority of the diocesan church over the national. Bolt provides a side bar to the idea of 'reception' within the Anglican Church by which an innovation may require significant time to be accepted throughout the provinces. He is at pains to point out that if the innovation proves unacceptable, a process of 'reception' ought to allow it not to be 'received' by the communion, but rejected. Bolt places the ordination of women in the category of that which is unacceptable and ought to be rejected.

Stephen Spence, who begins his article with the surprising assertion that the Baptist Church does not exist, describes himself as a representative Baptist, but not a representative *of* Baptists. He undertakes from the outset to describe the nature of the dispersed authority of the Baptist Church as a means of explaining that there is, properly understood, no Baptist view of the ordination of women. He states that gender is not an issue for the south Australian Baptist Union with respect to suitability for ministry, but qualifies this with the recognition that local Baptist churches, who have autonomy in the appointment of pastors, rarely call a pastoral leader who is a female. Thus since 1974 there have been only three ordinations of women, and there is only one woman Baptist pastor currently in ministry in South Australia. Spence suggests that local resistance to women pastors is based on a biblical hermeneutic which views the Bible as an 'instruction manual'. Spence, who wishes to diverge from this particular hermeneutic, demonstrates that what Paul wrote about the position of women in the church is not addressing the pastoral office as it is understood today. In any case, Paul's connection between ordination and authority is not one easily reconciled to a contemporary Baptist sensibility that the conscience of the individual before God is the only authority. Spence postulates that the Baptist hermeneutic that he has identified is further problematic, as it attempts to read contemporary issues into the New Testament text. This amounts to forcing the text to answer questions it is not itself asking. Spence affirms the ministries of significant women in the New Testament Church who were co-workers with Paul. He even goes so far as to suggest that in the Roman Church, women ministers were more prominent than male leaders. Spence finishes by enjoining readers of scripture to be oriented not towards past models but towards a helpful eschatological future within which women can play their part.

Archbishop Phillip Wilson writes about the ordination of women from a Roman Catholic perspective. He sets the issue within three separate contexts. The first is that of an ecumenical concern for unity, which ultimately might find expression in an ecumenical petrine ministry. The second is the context of contemporary sensibilities about the equal dignity of women with men in their being and ministry. The third is a post- Vatican II reconceptualisation of communion, by which the ordained ministry can no longer 'absorb and monopolise the ministry of the whole community'. Against the background of these developing contexts, Archbishop Wilson affirms the position of the magisterium that it does not feel itself able to authorise the ordination of women to the priesthood as this would be in conflict with the universal tradition of the church which is founded on the word of God.

Josephine Armour begins her presentation with the words of that great and renowned Roman Catholic theologian Karl Rahner who established that there was no theological reason to give a negative answer to the question: can women be ordained? Armour argues that principles of life and love are exemplified in God the Holy Trinity. She maintains that if trinitarian theology is taken as the basis of how the Church is to be, this would open up the ordained ministry to all, irrespective of gender, and would remove from within the church tendencies towards hierarchicalism and towards the prioritisation of a centralised authority of a male celibate priesthood. Armour sees the Trinity as radically inclusive, and existing in a mutually expressed love which overflows to the creation. From this model of Trinity Armour derives a model for discipleship by which all baptised people would be involved in all ministries of the Church. And the various modes of ministry would be governed by ways of relating which display mutuality, collaboration, and non-hierarchical decision-making. In Armour's schema this would also pertain to the episcopate which would be non-authoritarian, would protect unity, but also diversity, as these are expressed and lived out in the life and ministry of the Church. Rather than being content with a gender-defined under-standing of the icon of Christ, Armour suggests that Christian women and men are together called to participate in the life of God by standing *in persona Christi*. Here the ontological gives way to the relational. Armour claims a place for democratisation of the church, and asks that all ministries be recognised as having a sacramental dimension.

A third Roman Catholic voice is expressed in John Collins' article. Collins wishes to remove the debate about women's ordination from the context of sacramental theology where it is usually found, to a new place within the theology of the ministry of the word, which he suggests provides common ground for women and men. Collins asserts that the central question is, 'can a woman not purvey this word as effectively as a man?' Collins claims that the answer is clearly 'yes' and that the justice for women called for by Mary Wollstonecraft as early as 1792 should be attainable in the Church.

Collins points up some of the main emphases occurring in the Roman Catholic debate about women's ordination. He acknowledges that there are those who do not support the ordination of women, as they would not want women to collude with models of ministry strongly reflective of 'priestly sacerdotalism'. A contested area surrounds claims about the distinctive natures of women and men which emerge from what Collins considers a distorted anthropology, but which, perplexingly, were reinforced by certain pronouncements of John Paul II. A second contested area is the place of women in the ministry of the early church. Whilst suggesting that scholarship in this area is inconclusive, Collins nevertheless acknowledges the prominent place women played in the ministry of the church in Paul's time. He sees the constraining of women to have taken place around three generations later under a Greco-Roman influence that restricted women to the domestic sphere.

A third contested area is the place of women in the writings of Luke. Did Luke portray women as central to ministry in the early Church or, as some suggest, did he merely depict them in subordinated roles? Collins then returns to his paradigm of the theology of the word of God to assess the story from St Luke's Gospel of the woman with a flow of blood. From his reading of this story, Collins concludes not only that Luke supported women, but that we can derive the meaning that women too are able to give witness to the life of the word of God. And he suggests that the cries of justice of contemporary catholic women echo and give new voice to the witness of that prophetic woman from St Luke's Gospel.

Philip Kariatlis is the sole representative in this volume of the Orthodox tradition. Kariatlis states clearly that the Orthodox Churches oppose the ordination of women on the basis that it is a break with tradition. He emphasises that this does not reflect contempt for women, who, after all, have as their role model Mary, Jesus' mother, and who continue to be the 'soul' of the church in leading lives of love and sacrifice. Kariatlis outlines four main issues connected with women's ordination. One is that people see women having equal status with men in society and political life, and argue that this means the church should have women bishops and presbyters. In countering this, Kariatlis refers to the argument that neither Christ nor the early church appointed women to ordained ministry. The second issue is that maleness is indispensable for ecclesial leadership in the orthodox churches because of the biblical witness. The third issue is the establishment of a Christian anthropology which claims a distinct ontology for men and women posited on the idea that gender is an hypostasised expression of human nature. It is further argued that gender has hierarchical implications which give men priority over women. The fourth issue to be brought to bear on this debate is, Kariatlis claims, that of the iconic nature of the bishop/priest within orthodoxy that precludes women from involvement in ordained ministry.

Auxiliary arguments brought to bear within these four main themes are that even a counter-cultural Jesus did not make women leaders in the church; that gender is part of God's plan having been attributed to human beings before the Fall, and that gender is permanent being found as a distinct hypostasis without which realisation of personhood is an ontic impossibility. Kariatlis maintains that in God the Trinity resides a principle of 'hierarchical equality' and that this should be realised in the ordering of Christ's church on earth. Underlying these auxiliary arguments are themes such as that of headship and gender complementarity found elsewhere in this collection, and argued throughout the history of the women's ordination debate.

We are grateful to the contributors to this volume of *Interface*. The collection presents for the twenty-first century a representation of those arguments that have characterised the debate about the ordination of women during the preceding two centuries, but draws them into a contemporary context of changed social and political mores that represent a post-millennium consciousness. We commend this collection as a sound basis for the ongoing debate about women's ordination within Christian churches.

Cathy Thomson and Vic Pfitzner

Adelaide

First In Congregationalism: the Ordination Of Women In International Historical Perspective

Julia Pitman
Canberra

Women have been ordained in the Uniting Church in Australia since 1977 and in all three former denominations: Congregationalism from 1927, Methodism from 1969, and Presbyterianism from 1974. Historically the ordination of women in these three churches in Australia occurred relatively late when viewed in international perspective, and was reliant on the achievement of women's ordination in Congregationalism in Britain and America. In any current debate about the ordination of women in Christian churches in Australia, simply to provide an exegesis of the texts that have been used to support opposition to the ordination of women or even to speculate on how the ministry of women is received, would be to ignore the history of the ordination of women, which has spanned over 150 years and has now occurred in many Protestant denominations in countries around the world. An important part of this history involves accounts of debates about women's ordination, which often discussed St Paul's injunction that women should keep silent in church. Female theological students, who were asked to support their desire for ordination with biblical criticism, became the leading protagonists for women's ordination in their church, the women's movement, and the wider community. Their apologetic, which formed a significant part of their distinctive contribution to the Christian ministry, incorporated not only a modern exegesis of St Paul's writings, but also arguments for gender equality based on the creation narratives and themes within Reformed theology. Relying on the nineteenth century belief in the special ministry of women, they also argued that women would make a contribution to the Christian ministry that would be complementary to that made by men. The reception in both church and community of their apologetic for women's ordination improved over time, as did the reception of their ministry.

The following paper is limited to a brief overview of the history of women's ordination in the first denomination to ordain women, Congregationalism, with passing references to the experience of women in other denominations. It is also limited to three geographical contexts: America, where Antoinette Brown was ordained first in 1853, Britain, where Constance Todd was ordained during the First World War in 1917, and Australia, as an example of a settler society, where Winifred Kiek was ordained in 1927.

Congregationalism emerged from the English Reformation, becoming the dominant religious denomination in America, the third largest denomination in England and Wales, and only a minor, but nevertheless active and distinctive denomination in Australia. The congregational ideal was the gathered church of true believers, a notion which stood opposed to the ideal of membership in the Established Church of England, where all citizens, as members of the nation, were assumed to be members of the Church. However American Congregationalism followed the ideal of established churches with conformity in some northern states until the early nineteenth century. In England, the Restoration of the Monarchy in 1662 forced English and Welsh Congregationalism into dissent. Under the Toleration Act of 1689, Congregationalists were allowed to worship freely but they were not able to seek public office until the repeal of the Test and Corporation Acts in 1828. Colonists transplanted the ideal of independent churches into settler societies such as Australia, even if support for them was not very strong, and other Protestant denominations such as the Anglican, Methodist, and Presbyterian became much larger. Together with sympathetic Anglicans, British nonconformists ensured that no church became established in Australia.

Congregationalism as a denomination had several characteristics that predisposed it to ordain women first.[1] Its decentralised polity meant that the local church had authority over its own life including the call and ordination of a minister. In Congregationalism, the call of a minister was more important than ordination, allowing women access

---

1. Mark Chaves, *Ordaining Women: Culture and Conflict in Religious Organisations* (Cambridge, Massachusetts: Harvard University Press, 1997). Fuller documentation for the present paper can be found in Julia Pitman, *Prophets and Priests: Congregational Women in Australia, 1991–1977* (PhD thesis, University of Adelaide, 2005).

to the lay pastorate.[2] By the late nineteenth century, the denomination had developed a relatively strong tradition of liberal or non-conservative theological education, which also generated support for women's ordination in the church more generally. Congregationalists also differed from Anglo-Catholic and Catholic traditions, for while the Congregational churches saw themselves as the local expression of the universal church, they did not adhere to that aspect of sacer-dotalism, which insists upon the notion that a man must administer the sacraments in order to offer validly the sacrifice of Christ at the Last Supper. The movement for women's ordination also developed in relation to a wider women's movement, which had a religiosity of its own and advocated reform within religious denominations. Within their denomination, Congregationalists developed an autonomous women's movement, in which women developed the skills that would be required of ordinands: biblical interpretation and preaching, organisation, and decision-making capacities.

America[3]

Antoinette Brown was born into a family that valued education and she entered Oberlin Collegiate Institute, Ohio, in 1846. She received no encouragement from her tutors to enter the ministry, she was not permitted to speak in preaching class and her tutors even used her presence in class to support traditional gender roles. They asked her to justify why she wanted to become a minister by interpreting St Paul's injunction that women should be silent in church. Though designed to be a trial, this exercise sharpened Brown's ability to defend her desire to preach, which she would promote through the women's movement from 1850. Such biblical interpretation, which would become a feature of the ministry of women in America, Britain, and Australia into the twentieth century, helped women who lived in these countries to

---

2. John H Taylor, 'Ordination Among Us', *Transactions of the Congregational Historical Society*, vol 20, no 7, May 1968, 210–222; John Huxtable, 'Ordination: Aspects of a Tradition', *Journal of the United Reformed Church History Society*, vol 2, no 4, October 1979, 94–107.

3. The following section relies heavily on Beverly Zink-Sawyer, *From Preachers to Suffragists: Woman's Rights and Religious Conviction in the Lives of Three Nineteenth-Century American Clergywomen* (Louisville; London: Westminster John Knox Press, 2003).

critique religious arguments that conservatives used to support the subordination of women. In particular, proponents of women's ordination would use Brown's notion that St Paul's words were culturally contingent to his own time and not relevant to theirs.

Brown's essay, which she worked on in the winter and spring of 1848, was published in the *Oberlin Quarterly Review*. In this and later writings, she argued for two passages, 1 Corinthians 14: 34–35 and 1 Timothy 2: 11–12, to be considered within their own particular historical context and the literary context of the whole biblical canon. She argued for the equality of men and women as expressed in Genesis and Galatians 3:28. She also argued that for a man to assume headship of a wife was idolatrous, but that neither women nor men should teach in an authoritarian manner. For Brown, the Corinthians and Timothy passages in particular warned against abuses, both of leadership and of the response of the congregation to leadership. There was no actual prohibition against women preaching, she argued, and the epistles provided evidence that women were, in fact, leaders within the early church. According to the Corinthians passage women who were less educated than the men naturally asked questions which were better asked at home. A woman was 'merely told not to talk unless she does teach . . . the apostle says to the whole Church, woman included, "Ye may all prophesy, one by one".'[4]

Antoinette Brown had difficulty gaining a call to a pastorate and maintaining her ministry, initially because of her gender, but once she was in ministry, because of differences of opinion with her parishioners about theology. She was called to South Butler Congregational Church in the spring of 1853 and was ordained on 15 September. Unlike the lengthy debates about women's ordination that occurred in the twentieth and twenty-first centuries, there was little debate about her ordination, but also little support: her colleagues from other nearby Congregational churches did not attend the ceremony and Luther Lee, who gave the ordination sermon, would later refuse to sign a statement to the effect that he had ordained her. Brown argued for the ordination, first in relation to the needs of her own congregation, then herself, and then in relation to the position of women more generally:

---

4. Elizabeth Cady Stanton, Susan B Anthony and Matilda Joslyn Cage editors, *History of Woman Suffrage*, vol 1, (6 vols; Rochester, New York: National American Woman Suffrage Association, 1881, 1922), 536.

'It will do them good, and me good, & good to the cause of woman'.[5] The Reverend Luther Lee offered the ordination sermon, which reflected the Congregational view of an ordinand as a lay person set apart from the congregation who was already prepared for ordination by God and study, rather than through any effect of the service itself.

By the summer of 1854, Brown had left the ministry and avoided membership of a denomination until 1878, when she joined the Unitarian Church. For Olympia Brown, who entered St Laurence University Theological School Canton, New York in 1861 to train for the Universalist ministry, Antoinette Brown Blackwell's 'example' had been 'in a measure lost'.[6] While Brown Blackwell used theological criticism to support her ordination, Olympia Brown, by contrast, introduced a second, pragmatic argument that would become popular in arguments for women's ordination in the twentieth century, that of the special nature of women and their experience as wives and mothers. Olympia Brown had a better experience than Brown Blackwell as a minister of a congregation, with her ministry lasting twenty-five years. But like many of the first women ordained in America, Olympia Brown would move into full-time work for women's suffrage. This change was not simply related to gender discrimination in the ministry, which varied over time and place, but was a direct response to the first women ministers' experience of pastoral care among women, as well as the growing momentum of the movement for women's suffrage. Olympia Brown, Antoinette Brown Blackwell, and Anna Howard Shaw, the first woman ordained in Methodism in 1880, would all see their devotion to the cause of women's suffrage as an extension of their Christian ministry.

Like the situation today, Christian women in the mid-nineteenth century had a complex and ambivalent relationship to the wider women's movement, often considering themselves caught between the anti-clericalism and anti-ecclesiasticism of the women's movement on the one hand, and the conservatism of their own churches on the other. But Brown Blackwell, Olympia Brown, and Shaw submitted their misgivings to the belief that women's suffrage was the means to realise

---

5.   Antoinette Brown Blackwell to Gerrit Smith, 23 August 1853, recorded in Elizabeth Cazden, *Antoinette Brown Blackwell* (Old Westbury, New York: Feminist Press, 1983), 77.

6.   Olympia Brown, *An Autobiography*, edited by Gwendolen B Willis, *Annual Journal of the Universalist Historical Society* 4 (1963): 25.

their religious vision of gender equality. They were asked to pray and preach at women's suffrage meetings, becoming popular orators, and their title 'Rev' was always included in the records of women's suffrage organisations. Their contribution to the women's suffrage movement was recorded in the history of it written by Elizabeth Cady Stanton, Susan B Anthony, and Matilda Joslyn Cage. In turn, the women's movement influenced the rhetoric of women ministers with Brown Blackwell arguing, in 1874:

> She whom Nature especially enjoins to self-forgetfulness must be allowed to remember all other needs, those nearest at hand, those most remote . . . The natural mother of little children is also the natural mother of nations.[7]

Of the three women ordained first in America, Anna Howard Shaw most clearly expressed the connection between her experience as a minister in pastoral care situations and the need for women's suffrage. In addition to her training in theology, Shaw became a medical practitioner and worked in the Boston slums. She worked tirelessly as President of the National American Woman Suffrage Association during the lean years of the women's suffrage movement from 1904 to 1915 and would become a peace activist during the war, becoming the first woman to win the Distinguished Service Medal in May 1919. She argued, 'The time has come when we will no longer sit quietly by and bear and rear sons to die at the will of a few men'.[8] Her motivation for suffrage work had come from her experience of the Boston slums, where she felt powerless to assist women who were trapped in poverty.

The first women ordained in America saw women's suffrage as an extension of their ministry, as a means to realise their vision for a new world in which men and women would be equal. Having witnessed the effects of poverty and domestic violence on women, they believed that women's suffrage would not only raise the standard of living for women but, by doing so, transform society as a whole. Antoinette

---

7.　Antoinette Brown Blackwell, 'Work in Relation to the Home—IV', *Woman's Journal*, 23 May 1874, 161.

8.　Anna Howard Shaw, 'What the War Meant to Women' (League to Enforce Peace 1919), 18.

Brown Blackwell lived to cast her ballot in the first national election open to women on 2 November 1920, aged 95. She died the following year. By 1920, nineteen Protestant churches had begun to ordain women, including the African Methodist Episcopal Zion Church, which ordained the first African-American woman in 1898. The Association of Women Preachers (est 1919) was founded to raise awareness of the need for women's ordination in those denominations that did not yet ordain women. The organisation continues to this day as the International Association of Women Ministers and, since 1921, has published a journal, the *Woman's Pulpit*.

Britain

Historical research into women's ordination in English and Welsh Congregationalism is not as advanced as that for America, and the latest work is yet to be published.[9] The connections between women's ordination and the women's suffrage movement in Britain have not yet been explored thoroughly. As the influence of Puritanism and Revivalism was less apparent in Britain than in America by the mid-nineteenth century, the first woman was not ordained in Britain until 1917. Women ministers therefore did not take an active role in the women's suffrage movement and did not enter into the annals of its history in the way that they did in America. Women preachers participated in both the movement for women's ordination and the movement for women's suffrage. They shared American women ministers' concern for political equality for women from their experience of pastoral care. The Church of England and the Free Church Suffrage Leagues (est from 1909) were not only important sources of popular support for women's suffrage, but also the 'cradle of women's ordination in Britain'.[10] In turn, the preacher and suffragist Hatty Baker saw women's ordination as: 'the nearest way to the poll'.[11]

---

9. Elaine Kaye, Janet Lees, and Kirsty Thorpe, editors, *Daughters of Dissent* (London: United Reformed Church, 2004). Kirsty Thorpe is writing further on this topic.

10. Jonathan Inkpin, 'Combatting the "Sin of Self-Sacrifice": Christian Feminism in the Women's Suffrage Struggle (1903-1918)', (PhD thesis, Department of Theology, University of Durham, 1996), 383.

11. *Votes for Women*, 13 September, 796.

The Church Suffrage Leagues provided a vehicle for consciousness raising and lobbying for women's ordination and women's suffrage in the context of significant opposition from within Congregationalism to women's leadership. In May 1912, for example, the Free Church Suffrage League passed a resolution condemning the inaction of the Free Church Council, which had failed to discuss women's ordination at its March meeting. Similarly, suffrage agitation about the churches' response to the women's suffrage movement increased from 1913, as suffragists sought support for women's suffrage from the pulpit and in prayers for intercession. When these requests were not granted, women interrupted services to say their own prayers from the pews in several Anglican churches and to call out questions to the Rev RJ Campbell at the City Temple, the Mother Church of Congregationalism, in 1913.[12] Women also started women-only churches and services.

Hatty Baker was one of the most prominent women admitted to the lay pastorate in twentieth century English and Welsh Congregationalism, and held pastorates first at Mrs Martindale's Church at Horsted Keynes, then at Brighton, and then at Plymouth. She was also the first secretary of the Free Church League for Women's Suffrage, formed in 1910. Baker, who was shocked at the opposition to women preachers she encountered in her own church, was the first woman preacher at the inauguration of the Church of the New Ideal, a church that promoted Gnostic ideas, published a journal called *Urania*, and held services for women-only on Sunday evenings. Baker promoted the equality of men and women in ministry in order to represent the 'Mother-Father God' to the churches. She noted the dissatisfaction of women with pastoral care from male ministers who 'either ignore women altogether in essentials, or praise and encourage them in things which do not in the least matter nor help them to develop a true self'.[13] Baker also weighed into criticism of the secularisation of the suffrage movement, arguing that women suffragists would support a church that admitted women to leadership who would thus provide a female perspective on Scripture and social policy. While church services 'remained in old ruts and grooves . . . it had no message for them', she said. Baker did not proceed to ordination in Congre-

---

12. *Suffragette*, 17 October 1913, 6.
13. *Suffragette*, 19 December 1913, 225.

gationalism as she did not complete the required theological education, although she was referred to as 'Reverend'.

Constance Todd was ordained in 1917 and married Claude Coltman, a fellow Congregational minister, at a service the following day. Constance Todd's experience of ministerial education was quite different from that of Antoinette Blackwell Brown in America, who had read theology over sixty years earlier. Todd entered Mansfield College in 1913, where she found that, after her male peers had discussed her presence in the college, they found that they had no objection to her attendance at sermon classes and to her preaching. She chaired a conference for students on preaching and invited as speaker Maude Royden, a suffragist, peace activist, and candidate for the ministry in the Church of England who would become Assistant Minister to Dr Fort Newton at the City Temple from 1917 to 1920. Constance Todd was ordained to Darby Street Mission, a lowly-paid mission of the King's Weigh House, in a joint ministry with her husband. She saw marriage as 'yet another qualification' for ministry. She focused her attention on pastoral care, baptisms, and weddings, while her husband focused on preaching and chairing meetings. Coltman found in the ministry a retreat from suffrage work, for while speaking as a suffragist, she and Maude Royden had been shouted down by crowds at Hinckley. But she maintained her involvement in the women's movement, as a speaker and liturgist. For example, on the night of the extension of the franchise to women under thirty, 21 February 1918, Free Church women held a service of celebration and thanksgiving in Queens Hall. Constance Coltman and Mrs Bonwick led the service, while Maude Royden preached. Coltman advocated for the ministry of women with the argument that lay people would want choice in the gender of the minister if they sought pastoral care from the church and that women ministers would strengthen support of the churches for peace. Both Coltman and Dorothy Wilson, who was ordained at Carrs Lane Congregational Church, Birmingham in 1927, testified that in pastoral care situations women confided in them matters that they were not prepared to discuss with a male minister.

By 1936, seventeen women had been ordained within English and Welsh Congregationalism, with some women switching from Presbyterianism or Methodism to be ordained. The first woman ordained in Wales was Suzie Rankin in 1925, and the first woman ordained in the Congregational Union of Scotland was Vera Kenmure in 1928. Many of the women ordained before the Second World War would be influenced by the thought of Maude Royden, who in 1929 established the interdenominational organisation, the Society for the Ministry of Women, which included women in the Commonwealth. Royden argued that women ministers would bring to church life a new interpretation of God's revelation to the world. Links with American women ministers were maintained by women such as Florence Frost-Mee, who was particularly active in the International Association of Women Ministers, serving on its executive. Only after the Second World War would black women become ordained. Madge Saunders was commissioned as a deaconess in the Presbyterian Church of England in 1966 and served for ten years at St James Presbyterian Church, Scott Road, Sheffield, before returning to Jamaica where she was ordained in 1976. By the time of the creation of the United Reformed Church in 1972, one hundred women had been ordained in Congregationalism. The first black woman minister ordained in the United Reformed Church was Marlene Brown, who was ordained in 1997.

Australia

In Australia, women's ordination occurred after the vote had been won and after the First World War. The rhetoric of Australian Congregational women ministers was therefore informed by the need to educate women to perform their roles as citizens and to educate the church more broadly about the effects of poverty, domestic violence and sexual abuse on women and about their vulnerability as wives, mothers, and civilians in modern warfare. Australian Congregational women ministers shared the concerns of women ministers overseas: the need for a feminist perspective on Scripture and social policy to be heard in the church, and for lay people to be able to choose a woman if they sought pastoral care from the church. These ministers reflected on Christ's special ministry toward women and mined the Bible for references to women as examples of discipleship that modern women could emulate. Their attempt to inform their church with a feminist perspective on social policy had some success.

Winifred Kiek was ordained at Colonel Light Gardens Congregational Church on 13 June 1927. She studied theology at Parkin College Adelaide from 1923, training under her husband, ES Kiek, who was Principal. She completed an MA in Old Testament Languages and Literature in the 1920s. Violet Callanan was the first woman ordained in the Churches of Christ in 1931.[14] In Methodism and Presbyterianism, the popular move towards the creation of the order of deaconess after the Second World War, was a concession to the movement for the ordination of women. The deaconesses were commissioned, not ordained, and were subordinate to male ministers. Most of the first women ordained in the Methodist and Presbyterian churches, which ordained women from 1969 and 1974 respectively, had been deaconesses. Fifteen women were ordained in Congregationalism from 1927 until the creation of the Uniting Church in 1977. In both Britain and Australia, the introduction of a national stipend as a result of the formation of the union churches addressed the inequality in pay and conditions that women ministers had experienced in Congregationalism, which had offered ministers individual contracts. The expectation that women would be ordained in these new churches meant that women ministers were relatively accepted by congregations.[15] The first indigenous woman ordained in Australia was the Rev Liyapidiny Marika, ordained in the Northern Synod of the Uniting Church in September 1991.[16]

Congregational women ministers became advocates for women from other denominations seeking to enter the ministry, both within the ecumenical movement and the women's movement. The International Association of Women Ministers and the Society for the Ministry of Women sought to work for women's ordination in other denominations. British Congregational women ministers played a role in supporting women ministers from Europe and the Caribbean, and Australian women supported women who lived in areas where the London Missionary Society was active, viz in Africa, Asia, and the Pacific. Constance Coltman, for example, who was the only woman minister to be appointed Vice-President of the Society for the Ministry of Women, learned Swedish to encourage the movement for the ordination of women in Sweden, which was achieved in 1960. In Australia, the funds provided by the Winifred Kiek Scholarship supported Violet Sampa, the first woman ordained in Zambia, to come to Australia for further theological education and ministry experience.

14. W Tabernee, 'Women and Pastoral Ministry in Churches of Christ', *Church Scene* 519, 6.
15. Edward C Lehman, *Women in Ministry: Receptivity and Resistance* (Melbourne: Joint Board of Christian Education, 1994).
16. *Insights*, March 2005, 4.

But in their advocacy for women's ordination, women ministers such as Kiek inadvertently may have reinforced the expectation that such advocacy was women's work, that a 'double burden' for women in ministry was acceptable. The expectation that women ministers should perform their tasks better than men, was found in all three case studies, as was the finding that women ministers had trouble managing home and work duties because they believed that they should be able to combine their ministry with traditional gender roles.

Biblical interpretation that supports the subordination of women as well as the real experience of domestic violence and war remains with us, affecting society as a whole. Equality between women and men in ministry and the presentation by the church of the perspective of women remains a matter for the entire Christian church. Women's ordination occurred first in Congregationalism because of the particular polity and theological position of the church. The experience of the first women ministers in America was that after varied pastorates, they left the ministry to pursue women's suffrage in the hope that it would realise their religious vision of gender equality. In Britain, the ordination of women coincided with the women's suffrage movement and the First World War, making women's citizenship and peace a major theme of the ministry of the first women ordained. In Australia, where women's ordination followed the vote, Congregational women ministers sought to educate women to be good citizens, hoping that Australia, as a nation without an Established Church, would provide an example of women's ordination to the world. The number of Congregational women ordained as ministers remained small, however. Though Winifred Kiek argued that the 'idea that a woman is unfit to speak in church because it is a consecrated building cannot be widely held in this land of freedom today',[17] conservative theological views in other denominations have proved resilient until relatively recently.

In all three countries, the advocacy of women for women's ordination arguably has become an added expectation of women ministers, rather than as a gift to the church. This advocacy for women's ordination should not be the responsibility of women ministers only. It remains but one part of a larger task for both women and men—that of Christian ministry, broadly defined.

---

17. *White Ribbon Signal,* 1 May 1933, 92.

'It Has Become Clear to Us . . .': The Justification of the Ordination of Women to the Ministry of the Word in the Uniting Church in Australia

Geoff Thompson
Brisbane

1. Introduction

> The Uniting Church in Australia ordains both women and men to the ministry of the Word. In doing so, we recognize that these men and women are called by God to preach the gospel and preside at the sacraments. We are concerned, however, that this is not yet the practice of the whole Church. We are deeply concerned about this, because *it has become clear to us* that the ordination of both men and women is a fundamental implication of the Gospel.[1]

Thus begins the official document, adopted in 1990, which establishes the grounds on which the UCA is committed to the ordination of women, 'Why does the Uniting Church in Australia Ordain Women to the Ministry of the Word?' The UCA inherited from its predecessor churches a commitment to the ordination of women which involved the setting aside of both traditional practices and a certain strand of biblical teaching. As such, it attracts two different lines of criticism. From the Catholic and Orthodox directions the UCA draws the criticism that in this regard it has acted in a typically *Protestant* and

---

1. Social Responsibility and Justice Committee of the Assembly Commission for Mission, *Why does the Uniting Church in Australia Ordain Women to the Ministry of the Word* (Sydney: Uniting Church Assembly, 1990), 3 (my emphasis). Hereafter references to this document will be cited in the main body of the text as *WMOW*, page number)

schismatic disregard of tradition. From a more conservative Protestant angle it is charged with a typically *liberal* Protestant disregard of the Bible.

The position adopted in *WMOW* would, however, reject both criticisms on the grounds that it is 'at last acting on an imperative that was part of the gospel of Christ from the beginning' (*WMOW*, 6). This position was not adopted in a cavalier way. It is rather the case that the church has tested the experience of women being called to this ministry by a particular configuration of Scripture and tradition in which the content of each and the relationship between them is governed by the hermeneutic of the gospel. On this foundation, the Uniting Church has been able to say, 'It has become clear to us' that the ordination of women is a fundamental implication of the gospel.

Nevertheless, in the fifteen years since *WMOW* was adopted some of the scholarly discussion of Scripture, tradition, the relationship between them, the exegetical methods used in *MWOW* to interpret Scripture, and ordination itself have been subject to new influences and pressures. This makes it timely to revisit the arguments proposed in *WMOW* and to test their stability and coherence.

To address these issues this paper will begin with a summary of the arguments made in *WMOW*, following which it will offer a re-assessment of those arguments in the light of several critical issues which could be seen to exert some pressure on them.

2. The key arguments of WMOW

As already indicated, the three churches which united to form the UCA in 1977 were already committed to the practice of ordaining women to the ministry of the Word. The continuation of this commitment within the UCA was stated in a strikingly matter of fact way in the *Basis of Union*.[2] Nevertheless, although significant theological discussion and inquiry had preceded the adoption of the practice in the uniting churches long prior to union,[3] *WMOW* represents the UCA's own developed defence of the practice. It was occasioned by a degree of confusion within the UCA, and by the need to present the UCA's case to its ecumenical partners. The argument is multi-layered, but for the purposes of this paper its three key features

---

2.   See paragraph 14 of the *Basis of Union* at http://nat.uca.org.au /basisofunion/Basis1992.htm.

3.   See *WMOW*, 6-9.

will be highlighted: the interpretation of Scripture, the priority of Scripture over tradition, and the representative nature of ordained ministry.

2.1 The interpretation of Scripture

In keeping with the UCA's foundational statement about Scripture in the *Basis of Union*, the engagement with the biblical material presupposes that there is no simple, unqualified identity between the texts of the Bible and the word of God. This, however, should not be interpreted as a disregard for the Bible: 'Our own position is . . . that our ultimate authority is not the letter of scripture but rather Christ himself, the living Word of God, to whom scripture bears witness and who speaks through it' (*WMOW*, 25).[4]

The interpretative strategy employed in *WMOW* will be familiar to all those engaged in the debate about the ordination of women. Drawing largely on the insights of the historical criticism of the Bible, the various historical and literary strata of the New Testament are distinguished from each other. From this emerges an historical and theological narrative according to which the early inclusion of women in leadership gives way to their exclusion from it. Hermeneutical priority is given to Jesus' 'striking and unusual' (*WMOW*, 12) equal treatment of women. This is then taken to be faithfully interpreted and reflected in Paul's teaching about the 'transcending' of the order of creation in Gal 3:38 (see *WMOW*, 15–17). This particular verse is, in fact, taken to represent a direct link between the gospel and the identity and form of the church: 'Trying to found the church's life on distinctions that have forever been declared void by Christ would be to reject the gospel altogether' (*WMOW*, 16). Having argued for the theological and chronological priority of this understanding of the male-female relationship practised by Jesus and taught by Paul, it is used to interpret and subordinate alternative or contradictory positions in both the Pauline and post-Pauline literature (see *WMOW*, 18–25).[5] The kinds of argument employed here are well known: contradictions

---

4.   So, the opening sentence of par 5 of the Basis of Union: 'The Uniting Church receives the books of the Old and New Testaments as unique, prophetic and apostolic testimony, in which it hears the Word of God and by which its faith and obedience are nourished and regulated.'

5.   At issue are the passages usually discussed in this context: 1 Cor 11:2–16; 1 Cor 7; 1 Cor 14:33b–36; Col 3:18f; Eph 5:22–33; 1 Pet 3:7; 1 Tim 2:11–15; Tit 2:3–5; 1 Tim 5:3–16.

in Paul are exposed, the ambiguity of the appeals to the order of creation is noted, and the cultural accommodation evident in the household codes of the Pastoral Epistles is identified. It is important to stress that the position adopted does not consist of removing or disregarding certain passages merely because they offend modern sensibilities: a serious attempt is made to argue from the gospel of Christ. So:

> If it could be shown, however, as we believe it can, that some of the New Testament utterances on the role of women in the Church arise directly from reflection on the gospel, whereas others are prompted primarily by a prudential concern for the Church's image in society, then priority should surely be given to the former. We have found examples of the latter kind of utterance in the Pastoral Epistles. . . Paul's dominant theme, on the other hand, is different: this is what God has done in Christ; this is what you *are* because of what God has done; now go and live it out in all your relationships (*WMOW*, 25).

Thus is the biblical justification made for the Uniting Church's reformation of the church's traditional practice of a male-only ordination.

2.2 The subordination of tradition

That the UCA felt constrained to depart from the 'almost universal practice of the church throughout most of its history' (*WMOW*, 5) should not, in principle, be altogether surprising. Standing in the tradition of the Reformed and Evangelical churches,[6] the UCA has appropriated the conviction deeply held within those churches that the church is manifestly capable of perpetuating—even for very long periods of time—practices which even if glossed with the mantle of 'tradition' can nevertheless come to be exposed as at worst sinful and at best as distortions of the gospel. Even to express the matter in these terms is, of course, to acknowledge that 'there is a fundamental difference between Reformed tradition and some other traditions

---

6. For the manner in which these traditions are understood to make a continuing claim upon the UCA see paragraph 10 of the *Basis of Union*.

concerning the relationship between church traditions and the Gospel' (*WMOW*, 28).

The issue of tradition is dealt with most explicitly in *WMOW* when it briefly summarises the patristic testimony against the ordination of women—testimony which obviously carries great authority in the Roman and Orthodox churches. The validity of the arguments of the Fathers themselves is questioned on the ground that because the arguments were based on the scriptural precedents they are vulnerable to the same gospel critique applicable to the biblical precedents themselves. As such, the authority of the Fathers is set aside, not just because of some generic (and simplistic) Scripture principle, but because *MWOW* maintains the Fathers were reading the Bible in the wrong way. 'If we read the same Bible that they read and come to different conclusions, it is because we read the Bible not as book of commands and precedents, but as apostolic witness to Christ' (*WMOW*, 28). This, it has to be admitted, is a somewhat reductionist account of the Fathers' use of the Bible. Nevertheless, it does reflect the fact that the UCA's commitment to the priority of Scripture over tradition also involves a particular way of reading Scripture, that is, as witness.

The appeal to tradition which draws on the tradition's 'constancy' is also questioned. With the help of a background reference to Karl Rahner, the appeal to the 'constant tradition' is queried on the grounds that 'the length of a belief or practice in the Church does not in itself make that belief or practice part of the Church's normative tradition' (*WMOW*, 29). This of course brings us back to the question of what is the Church's norm. Where other traditions take their cues for the ordering of the church from the Fathers or from the explicit teaching of the New Testament, the UCA begins its ecclesiological reflection with what it understands is the gospel itself:

> When we ask ourselves how to order the life of the church today, the <u>fundamental</u> question for us is therefore <u>not</u>, 'What did the New Testament writers think about this?' nor 'How did the New Testament Church order <u>its</u> life?' although of course there is much to be learned from that. The fundamental question for us today, and for every period of history is rather, 'What is the gospel of Jesus Christ?' This is then followed by 'What does the gospel imply for the

ordering of the church?' (*WMOW*, 10; underlining in
original).

When the answer to that question conflicts with a received
tradition, it will be the received tradition which must yield. So it is the
case, so far as the UCA is concerned, with the tradition of ordaining
only males to the ministry of the Word.

2.3 Ordination and priestly representation

The issue comes to focus in the claim from the Catholic and Orthodox
traditions that the priest is an *ikon Christi*, and for that reason is
necessarily male. The issue is dealt with quite briefly, and *WMOW*'s
objections to it are those which are conventionally made to this
argument. The argument is novel; Christ is defined by more than his
maleness (and therefore pushed to its limit any representation of Christ
should also share those other features); and Christian salvation has
rested on Christ's assumption of the human condition *per se*. This last
point is made as follows: John's gospel says that 'the word became *sarx*
[flesh]'. So the Nicene Creed affirms that for us humans [*anthropous*],
the Son became human [*sarkothenta*] (*WMOW*, 31).

What is perhaps most noteworthy in *MWOW*'s rejection of this
doctrine is the fact that it does not seek to subvert it, as populist
Protestantism might, by objecting to the notion of priesthood *per se*.
Instead, it leaves the notion of priestly representation in place and
argues for the capacity of women to make such representation: 'Thus if
one took the view that the priest is an icon of Christ, it does not follow
that a woman cannot be such an icon simply because she is a woman'
(*WMOW*, 31).

3. Challenges

I turn now to the challenges that might be put to the arguments
presented in *WMOW*. Each of the three issues considered here predate
WMOW but could be said to have come to sharper focus in more recent
years.

3.1 Deconstructionism and historical criticism

In many ways, the position developed in *WMOW* is a classic case of
drawing theological conclusions, and initiating theological reform, on

the basis of knowledge drawn from the historical critical method.[7] Although long suspect within the church because of its 'deflationary'[8] effect on traditional Christian beliefs, historical criticism has nevertheless been implicated more recently in the broader postmodern criticism of modernity's pseudo objectivity. The particular challenge to be noted here is the literary challenge associated with deconstructionism.

Where the approach taken in *WMOW* is vulnerable to deconstructionism is the former's apparent confidence in the authority of origins. For one of the targets of deconstructionism is precisely the 'notion that meaning can be secured and decisively defined in discovering the most primitive layer of a text's historical life'.[9] Yet Christianity simply *is* governed by its origins, although not in any naïve historicist sense. For instance, the earliest strata of women's ministry is privileged in *WMOW* not because it is the earlier, but because it was judged to be the most congruent with the gospel. Historical criticism was used not so much to establish origins, but to open up the canonical text in such a way that its theological distinctions could be discerned and theological judgments made. To this extent it is the theologically diverse and diachronic nature of the canon that makes historical criticism a vital theological tool. It is for such reasons that Rowan Williams, for instance, has resisted the synchronic approach to biblical interpretation favoured by deconstructionism and has argued for the continuing legitimacy of diachronic readings, for which historical enquiry is obviously an indispensable tool.

> The movement of our canonical texts is frequently a
> quite explicit response to or rebuttal of some other
> position *within* the same canonical framework; the

---

7. This is of course a very broad term, and space allows only this generic use in the present paper. For an account of the range of approaches embraced by this term, see Alvin Plantinga, 'Two (Or More) Kinds of Scripture Scholarship', *Modern Theology* 14 (1998), especially 250–58.

8. *Ibid*, 243.

9. Rowan Williams, 'Historical Criticism and Sacred Text' in David F Ford and Graham Stanton (editors), *Reading Texts, Seeking Wisdom: Scripture and Theology* (London: SCM, 2003), 217.

world it opens to us is one of uneasy relationships and
discontinuities.[10]

The canon, he writes elsewhere, is 'visibly a collection of discrete
compositions; it abounds in cross-reference; . . . it displays an inner
literary history (narrative texts reworking other narrative texts, from
Chronicles and Kings to Matthew and Mark)'.[11] For precisely such
reasons, he argues, 'we cannot simply begin from a finished textual
synthesis'.[12] Thus, 'it is possible to see the history of rewriting as both
response to existing tensions and evasion of tensions. We are not
licensed to relegate earlier strata in a textual history to hermeneutical
irrelevance'.[13] Therefore, far from being vulnerable on account of their
dependence on historical criticism, the arguments of *WMOW*
demonstrate 'the movement of the canonical texts' and generate a
richer theological position—while doing greater justice to the nature of
the canon—than if the texts regarding women's ministry were treated
as a 'finished textual synthesis'.

3.2 Re-thinking Scripture and tradition
The privileging of Scripture over tradition always carries the risk of
isolating Scripture from tradition. The problem, as diagnosed by John
Webster, is located in the 'distortions introduced into Christian
theology of Scripture in the post-Reformation era by its dogmatic
mislocation'.[14] In reaction to Roman doctrines of papal authority,
Reformed theology forced the doctrine of Scripture 'to migrate to the
beginning of the dogmatic corpus' and 'to do duty as a foundational
doctrine'; it became 'a relatively isolated piece of epistemological
teaching'.[15] As such, Scripture itself became a relatively isolated
theological source. If, therefore, the privileging of Scripture over
tradition in *WMOW* is a symptom of this doctrinal error, is it the case

---

10. Rowan Williams, *On Christian Theology* (Oxford: Blackwell, 2000), 53.
11. Williams, 'Historical Criticism and Sacred Text', 221.
12. *Ibid.*
13. *Ibid.*
14. John Webster, '"A Great and Meritorious Act of the Church"? The
     Dogmatic Location of the Canon' in John Barton and Michael Wolter
     (editorss), *Die Einheit der Schrift und die Vielfalt des Kanons /The Unity
     of the Scripture and the Diversity of the Canon* (Berlin and New York:
     Walter de Gruyter, 2003), 95.
15. *Ibid.*

that the traditional practice of ordaining only men is less vulnerable to the biblically based critique than has so far been argued in this paper?

I believe not. For the corrective to this doctrinal error is not, in fact, to restore some allegedly lost balance between Scripture and tradition. It is, rather, to properly relate the doctrine of Scripture to other authoritative doctrines of the faith. This, I suggest, is precisely what is presented in the UCA's *Basis of Union.* What the *Basis* has to say about Scripture (in paragraph 5) derives its significance from what has already been said about Jesus Christ and the church (paragraphs 3 and 4).[16] The doctrine of Scripture is fully integrated with and cannot be separated from christology or ecclesiology. (This contrasts with present day fundamentalism which continues the doctrinal mistake of placing the doctrine of Scripture at the 'beginning of the dogmatic corpus', and making the authority of christology and ecclesiology dependent on a prior doctrine of biblical authority.) This is the ground, moreover, for establishing the gospel as the hermeneutical criterion of Scripture —precisely the strategy employed in *WMOW.*

At the same time, however, this integration and particular ordering of the various doctrines can be the grounds for re-casting the relationship between Scripture and tradition, by interpreting both of them by the gospel. It thus provides the UCA with solid grounds for upholding the tradition whilst distinguishing between the tradition and particular traditions. The tradition can be taken to be 'the gospel itself, transmitted from generation to generation in and by the Church'.[17] This is not merely the sum of the various traditions which the church has practised. As such the UCA can, in my view, defend its practice of ordaining women as being completely faithful to the tradition whilst being a departure from a particular tradition.

3.3 *Ordination and representation*

Although clearly stressing the problems with the idea of the priest as *ikon Christi,* *WMOW* left slightly open the possibility that this was a

---

16. Paragraphs 1 and 2 are largely historical and ecclesiastical pre-ambles to the event of union. Paragraph 3 is the first substantive doctrinal paragraph.

17. PC Rodger and L Vischer (editors), *The Fourth World Conference on Faith and Order, Montreal 1963,* Faith and Order Paper No 42 (SCM, London 1964), quoted in World Council of Churches Faith and Order, *Treasure in Earthen Vessels* accessed on February 4 2005 from http://www.wcc-coe.org/wcc/what/faith/treasure.html.

valid understanding of a representative priestly ministry. Against the view that such an understanding of priesthood necessitates a male priest, *WMOW* maintained on the basis of the soteriological nature of Christ's humanity that women could indeed fill precisely that role. Subsequent to *WMOW* the UCA was for other reasons[18] deeply engaged with the question of ordination itself. In those discussions the representative role was described in terms of the ordained minister's representation of the community before others, of the wider church before the local community, and, in a liturgical context, of Christ himself—'although all Christians share that responsibility'.[19] To some extent, this qualifier already restrains the investment the UCA might make in the *ikon Christi* debate. Given, however, that the UCA has explicitly spoken of the ordained minister's representative liturgical role, it will need to be able to respond to its ecumenical partners who use the *ikon Christi* argument to justify the ordination of males only to the priestly ministry.

Wider discussions about this concept have actually suggested that the idea itself is faulty, and that the representative role of ordained ministers is not best explained by it. TF Torrance, for example, allows that some notion of image or *ikon* might be retained, but only in its referential sense: 'not in its picturing or mimetic sense, but in its referential sense in which the image points beyond itself altogether and in so doing retreats entirely out of the picture'.[20] The theological issue at stake for Torrance is that any other understanding of the role of the celebrant threatens the substitutionary nature of Christ's sacrifice. '[A]t the altar the minister or priest acts faithfully in the name of Christ . . . only as he lets himself be displaced by Christ, and so fulfils his proper ministerial representation of Christ at the Eucharist . . . in which his own self, let alone his male nature, does not come into reckoning at all.'[21] Donald Mackinnon similarly insists on a non-mimetic role for the celebrant: 'The Eucharist is not', he writes, 'a Passion play in which the part of Jesus would need to be played by a male'.[22] Mackinnon,

---

18. Notably, the renewal of the diaconate.

19. The Assembly Commission on Doctrine, *Ordination and Ministry in the Uniting Church in Australia* (Sydney: UCA Assembly Standing Committee, 1994), 17.

20. Thomas F Torrance, *The Ministry of Women* (Edinburgh: T&T Clark, 1992), 10.

21. *Ibid*, 12.

22. Donald Mackinnon, 'The *Ikon Christi* and Eucharistic Theology', *Theology* XCV (1992): 110.

however, notes how the whole discussion of the identity and role of the celebrant deflects attention away from the elements—the promised locus of Christ's presence. The appeal to the *ikon Christi* 'seems . . . to suggest that Christ's real presence is to be sought neither in the action nor in the consecrated elements, but in the person of the priest.'[23] For Mackinnon this is a retreat from the 'objectivity characteristic of Catholic Eucharistic theology' according to which 'neither the disposition nor the beliefs of the celebrant invalidate the action'.[24] In short: 'The emphasis has shifted altogether from the bread and wine.'[25]

Although the references to priesthood, celebrant, and altar in these comments would jar for many in the UCA, the arguments presented here suggest that the UCA is better advised to question the *ikon Christi* understanding of priesthood rather than to endorse that understanding whilst insisting that women can fulfill it.

4. Conclusion

The interpretation of Scripture in *WMOW* and its particular understanding of the relationship between Scripture and tradition have been shown to withstand potential criticisms. Its openness to the appeal to the idea of the ordained minister as *ikon Christi* is less secure. The reasons mounted against this idea by other writers can nevertheless be added to the *WMOW*'s own reservations. In short, the reasons the UCA ordains women to the ministry of the word are neither trivial nor cavalier. If they involve setting aside some scriptural teachings, it is not because of a disregard for Scripture, but from a proper regard for the nature of the biblical witness and its relationship to the gospel. If they involve setting aside a particular tradition it is not through a disregard for the tradition but from a proper regard for the relationship between the gospel, the tradition and traditions. They are reasons that continue to justify the UCA's claim that 'it has become clear to us' that the ordination of women to the ministry of the Word is a fundamental implication of the gospel.

---

23.   *Ibid.*
24.   *Ibid.*
25.   *Ibid*, 111

Five Pillars That Totter and Crumble To Dust: Can Genesis 2 and 3 Support Subordination of Women?

Peter Lockwood
Adelaide

1. Introduction

Those who oppose the ordination of women in the Lutheran Church of Australia base their case on what they regard as God's revealed will that men take precedence over women in the church and the home. The rule of men, they say, comes to clearest expression in the two New Testament texts where women are forbidden to speak and teach in church (1 Cor 14:34,35; 1 Tim 2:11–14). Rather than exercising authority over men, women are to learn in silent submission. These texts, in turn, are said to presuppose male headship (Eph 5:22–24; 1 Cor 11:3), which has as its foundation in the creation and fall narratives of Genesis 2 and 3.[1]

Five main items drawn from Genesis 2 and 3 form a major part of the agenda of those who believe that it is not the place of women to take a leading role in worship by preaching and administering the sacraments:

- the prior creation of the man, coupled with the derivative creation of the woman (2:21,22)
- the woman's depiction as the man's helper (2:18,22)
- the allegedly greater culpability of the woman in the fall account (3:1-6)
- God's punishment of the woman by placing her under the

---

1. It is generally acknowledged that Genesis 1 provides little support for notions of male-precedence. Both men and women are God's image on earth (Gen 1:26–28; see also 9:6; James 3:9). Women, no less than men, are portrayed as the crown of creation. Both are intended for an intimate and harmonious relationship with God; they are co-regents with God, and as procreators they are vested with the honour of being co-creators with God.

dominion of the man (3:16)
- the man's two-fold naming of the woman (2:23; 3:20),
  confirming his position of authority

From these five pillars, read in the light of 1 Timothy 2:13,14,[2] it has been concluded that the Bible provides an hierarchical ordering of creation, establishing Eve's position as secondary and derivative and auxiliary. And the tradition of the church has confirmed this understanding of Eve's place in the scheme of things, the lot of women thereafter. How such notions became so deeply embedded in the Lutheran Church[3] can be more readily understood when one reads excerpts like this from Luther's 1536–1537 lectures on Genesis.

The rule remains with the husband, and the wife is compelled to obey him by God's command. He rules the home and the state, wages wars, defends his possessions, tills the soil, builds, plants, etc. The woman, on the other hand, is like a nail driven into the wall (Luther's Works 1:202).

Presupposing that the Genesis texts are foundational and normative for the biblical view of the relationship between men and women, this paper offers a close study of the relevant verses and assesses the Lutheran Church's traditional understanding in the light of the findings.

2. The woman is made second and is derived from the man

Adherents to traditional views of the role of women in the church focus on the prior creation of the man in Genesis 2. It is the first pillar that supports their position.

Adam was formed first, and so, according to biblical theology, he has the priority. He was the first born, the teacher, who received God's teaching about the need for obedience.[4]

---

2. 'Adam was formed first, then Eve; and Adam was not deceived, but the woman was deceived and became a transgressor' (1 Tim 2:13,14, NRSV).

3. A significant change in thinking in most parts of the Lutheran world was precipitated by Swedish theologian Krister Stendahl's *The Bible and the Role of Women: a Case Study in Hermeneutics*, first published in 1958. It appeared in an English translation in 1966.

4. '1 Corinthians 14:33b–38 and 1 Timothy 2:11–14 prohibit the ordination of women', *Lutheran Theological Journal* 39/1, May 2005: 59.

The appeal [at 1 Tim 2:13] to Adam's priority in Genesis 2 locates the basis for the command that women should not teach, *before* the fall.[5]

However, rather than regarding the woman as secondary because she is made second, it could also be argued that Eve is the crowning achievement of God's creation after the experiment of Adam. But that would be to err in the other direction. Or it could be argued that she is made of superior stuff to Adam, not soil but bone. Or attention could be drawn to the many stages involved in the creation of the woman (vv 21,22) as opposed to the simple two-step operation leading to the creation of the man (v 7), or the fact that she is not moulded as a potter moulds a clay figure, but built as a house or palace is built. The Hebrew word in verse 22, usually translated 'made', is the word 'built'. The scale of the operation is far grander and more elaborate. But all such arguments dwell too literally on the details of the story and fail to see what they are saying.

It is instructive in this connection to trace the plot, or story line, of the so-called second account of creation. After the repeated references to God's positive evaluation of his creation in Genesis 1 (vv 4,10,12,18,21,25,31), it is striking that the author of chapter 2 highlights two major downsides, one to commence the story (vv 5,6), and the other halfway through (vv 18–20). They are narrative complications that cry out to be resolved. At the commencement of the story the reader learns that the created realm lacks vegetation, rain and a farmer to till the soil; and midway through the story the reader learns of God's concern that the man is alone. In each case the Lord God takes the initiative in resolving the dilemma, and the resolution is marked by the threefold use of the verb 'to become'. The man becomes a living being, resolving the problem of there being nobody to till the soil (v 8), the river divides and becomes four branches, resolving the problem of there being no rain or vegetation (v 10), and the man cleaves to his wife so that they become one flesh, resolving the problem of the man being alone (v 24).

---

5. 'A case for the ordination of men only', *LTJ* 39/1, May 2005, 29. Those who trace the rule of the male to the prior creation of the man in Genesis 2 will not find a ready ally in Luther. He writes: 'If Eve had persisted in the truth, she would not only not have been subjected to the rule of her husband, but she herself would also have been a partner in the rule which is now entirely the concern of males' (Luther's Works 1:203).

Viewed in this way, the plot progresses relentlessly towards the resolution of major problems: no vegetation, no rain, no tiller of the soil, and no helper as the man's partner. The author shows no interest in an upwards movement towards the creation of the woman as a superior being, or a downwards movement towards her creation as an afterthought. The verb 'to become' reveals the punch-line. The story as a whole moves unerringly towards the man leaving his parents, clinging to his wife, and ultimately their becoming one flesh.

The woman's derivation from the man has to do with the fact that men and women are made for one another; they balance one another; they complement one another; they correspond to one another; each is the other's partner, or 'other half'. The story does not build towards the creation of the woman, but towards the man and woman becoming *one flesh* (2:24), overcoming the problem God confronted from the outset, 'It is not good that the man should be alone; I will make him a helper as his partner' (2:18). Narratively, the story rules out the conclusion that being created second means the woman is in any sense less than the man or subservient to him. Rather, the story drives without wavering towards the conclusion that men and women fit together wonderfully well according to God's creational design.

Another way of demonstrating the same point is by attending to the surface structure of the story. The structure of Genesis 2:4b–25 unfolds readily in broad outline.

> 1 The Lord God *forms the man* from the soil and breathes into him the breath of life (4b-7)
> 2 The Lord God plants a *garden* and places the man in it (8,9) X A *river* waters Eden and becomes four streams to water the earth (10-14) 2' The Lord God commands the man to till the *garden* and keep it (15-17) 1' The Lord God *builds the woman* from the rib and the two become one flesh (18-25)

The artist has drawn the couple in such a way that they are seen facing one another either side of the picture, rather than with one looking down upon the other. They are profoundly equal, while retaining their radical differences.

Extreme care must be taken regarding any conclusions drawn from the fact that the woman is made from the man's rib. Founding stories are crafted to reveal ultimate reality. The characters in this story could well have been switched, so that the man was built out of the woman's rib, and the message of radical mutuality and correspondence between the sexes would suffer no injury whatsoever. After all, what is said of the man—that he is formed from the dust—is equally true of the woman. Like the man she too will return to the dust from which she came (Ps 104:29; Job 34:14,15). Just as the common derivation of men and women from the soil symbolises their humanity and their mortality, the woman's derivation from the man's rib symbolises their partnership. The sequence is of no consequence.[6]

3. The woman is described as the man's helper (2:18,20)

The second pillar used to support the proposal that the woman is subordinate to the man in church and to her husband at home is her depiction as the man's helper. It is easy to assume that in offering to provide the man with 'a helper as his partner'. God has in mind little more than someone to ease the burden of the domestic workload and relieve the man's solitude. In English ears the word 'helper' conjures up images of someone to help with the household chores, an underling, even a paid employee.

Nothing could be further from the truth. The word 'helper' (*'ezer*) comes from the Hebrew word for protection, barrier or enclosure (*'azarah*). Of the twenty-one occurrences of 'helper' in the Old Testament, fifteen are used of God (eg Ex 18:4; Deut 33:7,26,29).[7] God is able to help precisely as the one who has made heaven and earth, provides the oppressed with justice and the hungry with food, releases prisoners, lifts up those who are bowed down, watches over strangers and protects orphans and widows (Ps 146:5-9, paraphrased).

When used of God, most occurrences of the words 'help' and 'helper' are found in a military setting. God is called helper when rescuing the people from their enemies by might of arms (Ps 124:8), so that a frequent metaphor for God is Israel's help and shield (eg Pss 33:20; 115:9,10,11). The psalms of lament provide frequent examples of the psalmist imploring God for help in the face of torment, danger, sickness or impending death (eg Ps 70:5; 79:9; 119:86), and other psalms express the quiet confidence that God can be relied on as a

---

6. Paul affirms that 'as woman came from man, so man comes through woman' (1 Cor 11:12).

7. For a helpful discussion of *'ezer* see the article by E Lipinski in TDOT XI, 12–17.

helper in times of difficulty and distress (Ps 121:1,2). The Hebrew word-group to which *'ezer* belongs suggests a degree of strength, support, and protection that is not captured by the English word 'helper',[8] even though the word is also employed in more every-day settings.[9] Given that the word 'helper' is used so often as a metaphor for God, or to portray the deeds of God, it is out of the question to suggest that the word could imply a secondary or subservient status when applied to women.

The God who helps humankind is the God who is characterised by community (see Gen 1:26). God longs for the man to belong within community also, and that community must be a community of equals. The author allows the reader to read God's mind, 'It is not good that the man should be alone'. Then and there God resolves to make him 'a helper as his partner' (2:18). God may well be humanity's helper, but the partnership is unequal, ill-matched. A helper is needed who corresponds to the man, who is equal to the man, who belongs with him inseparably, but preferably not one who is the same as him in all respects. This remarkable correspondence, this perfect fit, is captured by the compound prepositional phrase *kenegedu* (as his partner), more literally, 'as his counterpart', or 'as his opposite number'.[10]

Literary context provides the best way to determine the manner in which the man's 'other half' is meant to help him, and presumably he her. The propagation of the species does not enter the picture in Genesis 2 and 3, so that has to be ruled out. Prominent in chapter 2 are God's intentions that a farmer be found to till the soil and that, once

---

8.   Friedman (19) goes so far as to argue for an etymological connection between 'helper' (*'ezer*) and 'strength' (*'oz*).

9.   A couple of examples suffice. In face of the invading Assyrians, King Hezekiah gets his officers and soldiers to *help* him block up the wells and springs surrounding Jerusalem to make a long siege impossible (2 Chron 32:3). During the Babylonian exile, Second Isaiah derides the artisans, with their several trades, who *help* one another with words of commendation and encouragement as they construct their immovable idols (Isa 41:6,7).

10. The stress on correspondence and partnership is shown more clearly by comparing *kenegedu* and *lefanayw*, literally 'to his face', or 'before him', also used of people standing before one another. The compound prepositional construction *lefanayw* is used in a less direct sense, as in the Pope standing *before* the crowd in St Peter's Square, whereas *kenegedu* has the sense of two people eye-balling one another.

formed, the farmer not continue to live alone. Life in solitude is not life as God intended. Work and companionship, tilling and keeping the soil and being there for one another, are the dominant motifs in this captivating account. By creating the woman God has ensured that the man need live alone no longer. His loneliness is counteracted by female companionship. In this respect she has become his helper, and he hers.

But there is more. As counterparts to one another, that which applies to the man surely also applies to the woman. Both return to the dust from which they are formed, and men are made from women no less than the first woman was made from the first man. Accordingly, considering that the only task that is assigned in Genesis 2 is the task to till the soil and protect it, this must be seen as the shared responsibility of the man and the woman. If the earthlings are from the earth (humans from the humus, *adam* from *adamah*), and the only task they are assigned is to till (literally, serve) and protect the earth, that task is no less the responsibility of the woman than it is that of the man. In that respect also the woman is to be understood as the man's helper (contra Wenham: 68). Qoheleth ties together the two ways that Genesis 2 suggests that men and women help one another: 'Two are better than one, for they have a good reward for their *toil*. For if they fall, one will lift up the other; but woe to one who is *alone* and falls and does not have another to *help*' (Eccles 4:9,10).

4. The woman is more easily led astray, and more prone to lead others astray

The remaining three pillars used by the interpretative tradition in question derive from the fall account in chapter 3. The role that the woman plays in the story would appear to confirm her lesser place in the scheme of things. The serpent knew to engage her rather than the man in the diabolical dialogue (verses 1–5). After all, she represented the weaker sex (1 Pet 3:7). Luther repeats with approval the received opinion that 'the serpent was afraid of the male, as the master, and approached the woman; for although she herself was also holy, nevertheless, as the weaker creature, she was more likely to yield to persuasion' (LW 1:182). His words reflect a long and sorry tradition that regards women as more gullible than men, and therefore more susceptible to temptation.

To make matters worse, once she has fallen for the devilish deception the woman immediately leads the man astray (3:6). She is the arch-seductress, it is said, the temptress extraordinaire; and as was the woman in the garden, so also are women in general ever since.[11] Today the language is less harsh and the blame is distributed between Adam and Eve more evenly but, that aside, the sentiments are similar.

Eve usurped the spiritual headship of Adam by ceasing to be a student of her husband, while Adam dodged his responsibility to teach his wife by weakly following her teaching, with tragic cones-quences for both. So women were not to assume this role again, and the men were not to renege on it.[12]

The first part of the woman's punishment, which consists of the pain and hardship of child-bearing and childbirth (3:16a), is also said to prove her greater guilt. What she endures is far harsher than the man's sweaty brow as he tries to wrest his living from the stubborn and thorn-infested ground (3:17–19). Her body is affected in ways that men are not compelled to endure. But nothing highlights her greater culpability as much as the second half of her punishment, the permission given her husband to rule over her (Gen 3:16b). This is said to apply both in the home (Eph 5:22-24; 1 Pet 3:1,2) and in the church (1 Cor 14:34,35; 1 Tim 2:8–14). Women are to bow to the authority of their husbands at home, and silently learn from their instruction at church.

The Genesis text itself does not permit such a reading. It could as easily be argued that the man is more culpable than the woman, not less. After all, he was present throughout the diabolical conversation without intervening to prevent her from taking the forbidden fruit, and unlike her he takes and eats without so much as one word of protest (v 6). In addition, when called to account he places the blame both on the woman and God, whereas she finds only one scapegoat, the serpent

---

11. Tertullian said: 'Woman, you are the devil's doorway. You have led astray one whom the devil would not dare attack directly. It is your fault that the Son of God had to die; you should always go in mourning and in rags'. And Ambrose: 'Adam was led to sin by Eve and not Eve by Adam. It is just and right that woman accept as lord and master him whom she led to sin'. For copious references to early church theologians' opinions on gender relations, see Webb, 14–27.

12. 'Prohibit', *LTJ* 39/1, May 2005: 59. It is interesting to note in this quotation the rich overlay of opinions and value judgments—or to use the jargon, the extensive *eisegesis*. And given Luther's assertion that the man and the woman shared the rule before the fall (LW 1: 203), it is odd to hear it said that Eve usurped her husband's role as the one and only responsible teacher even before such a role had been assigned to him.

(vv 11–13). And if one were intent on determining greater and lesser fault, or thought that the text was interested in such matters, the fact that the man's punishment occupies three verses (v 17–19) as opposed to the woman's one verse (v 16) could not go unremarked.

The argument for greater culpability is read into the Genesis text from 1Timothy 2:13,14: 'Adam was formed first, then Eve; and Adam was not deceived, but the woman was deceived and became a transgressor'. Nowhere else does the New Testament suggest that Eve is at fault to a greater extent than Adam (Rom 5:12). Therefore it is all the more important to pay close attention to the historical, theological and pastoral contexts of these verses.[13]

The writer of the Pastoral Epistles was passionately concerned about the inroads that heretical teachers were making into the church at Ephesus. Some were arch legalists, others rampant libertarians, and the women at Ephesus were proving particularly vulnerable to the libertarians (1 Tim 2:8–15; 5:3–16; 2 Tim 2:6,7; Tit 2:3–5). In this context the author refers to the prior creation of Adam and the ready deception of Eve (1 Tim 2:13,14). Just as Adam received instruction from God first hand, so the men of the early church were for the most part better versed in the scriptures. Just as Eve received her instruction belatedly and second hand, so also the women of Ephesus were not so well grounded in the Torah due to the constraints placed on their sex by tradition and custom. Clear teaching in the church presupposes sound instruction, and the poorly instructed women proved an easy target for the charlatans who had insinuated themselves into the church; and it was chiefly the women who were eagerly promoting the false teachings.

The author's words are highly situation-specific. If they are lifted out of their immediate context and are applied more generally to the relationship of men and women, they vilify women as the more gullible and the more deceitful sex, and they totally distort, in fact they falsify, what Genesis 2 and 3 actually do have to say about gender relations.

5. God tells the woman that the man will rule over her (3:16)

Of the five pillars the fourth has been the most telling in the tradition. If God has punished the woman by subjecting her to the dominion of

---

13.   For a detailed exposition, see '1 Corinthians 14:33b–38 and 1 Timothy 2:11–14 permit the ordination of women', *LTJ* 39/1, May 2005: 66–83.

the man, then that should be the end of the story, with no questions asked. But the words call for close study. In narrative context the words God addresses to the serpent (3:15), the woman (3:16) and the man (17–19) are the sentences imposed for the guile of the serpent and the disobedience of the first parents. Defined in terms of genre, they are aetiologies. Cotter says the author is concerned about 'why snakes do not have legs, why people fear snakes, why childbirth hurts, why there is sexual desire, why men dominate women, why work is burdensome, why people die' (35). Presupposing the harsh realities of life as it is experienced in its infinite variety as a result of human sinfulness and a disordered world, the stories trace these realities back to their foundations in events of a bygone age, the disobedience of our first parents. One of these enduring realities is the dominance of men over women—in politics, in the work force and in the home.

Male rule is portrayed as punishment for the disobedience of the man and the woman in Eden. The age-old debate as to whether God's words to the woman, 'he shall rule over you', are a punishment or a perceptive description of the way things are in the world is a pointless exercise. The imperfect aspect of the Hebrew verb—in this case the verb *yimshol*—can function as a simple future and as an imperative, among other usages. Therefore the author can have the verb do double duty and mean both that the man 'will rule' and 'must rule' over the woman. The words are both descriptive and punitive, not one to the exclusion of the other.

Furthermore, the words addressed to the woman, 'he shall rule over you', need to be read together with the preceding words, 'your desire shall be for your husband'. They belong together. The two words 'desire' and 'rule' reappear together once more in the Cain and Abel story, providing a vital interpretative clue. God urges Cain to 'rule' or 'master' the sin that is lurking at his door, eagerly desiring to get the better of him (4:7). Two powerful forces are at loggerheads, Cain's evil desire to commit fratricide, and his better nature to which God makes an urgent appeal. Will the cruel beast and its ferocious desire have its way, or will God be able to tap into Cain's kind and forgiving heart? Cain is a battleground, and in no time the desire to do wrong prevails over the man's better nature.

Applying this to Genesis 3:16, may it not be that the woman's 'desire' is her desire to get the better of the man? She desires to overpower him in the same way that the desire to murder gets the better of Cain. But, sad to say, the man will invariably get the better of her. As indicated, this is punishment, but it is also a profound description of the way things will be as history unfolds. Men tend to be stronger than women in decisive respects—physically, politically, economically (1 Pet 3:7). Even though she will desire to gain the upper hand, the truth of the matter is that for the most part he will prevail, by virtue of brute strength. Here Genesis portrays for us the perennial battle of the sexes. In the face of impossible odds, women continue to try to get the better of men. With remarkable ease men seize and maintain control. The writer portrays the human condition with unerring accuracy.

This interpretation of the relationship between 'desire' and 'rule' was first proposed by Susan Foh (1974–1975). Since her article appeared commentators have felt a strange compulsion to make a decision—does the word 'desire' mean sexual desire or the desire to dominate (eg, Wenham: 82; Fretheim: 363). But the two are not necessarily mutually exclusive. Arguably it is more a case of the writer showing remarkable insight into gender relations, bedevilled as they are by bewildering complexity and ambiguity, consisting of fatal attraction despite male cruelty and multiple unwelcome pregnancies, and overlaid by episodes characterised by the impulse to strike back.

As punishment following the fall, is male dominance in the battle of the sexes to be regarded as God's immutable will for a fallen world? Few people regard the other punishments that follow the fall in those terms. The other sentences imposed are the pain of childbirth, the toil and sweat of agricultural work, and the thorns and thistles of the resistant soil. God does not decree these afflictions as his unyielding will, to which men and women are obliged to resign themselves. At every point it is regarded as perfectly legitimate to resist these results of the fall and reduce their harsh impact. Even though some believe the Bible forbids it, various forms of pain relief are offered to women in labour. Farmers do all they can to make the soil more productive and their working conditions more comfortable, even though this minimises the punishment God imposed from the outset. Surely the same applies to the second component in the woman's punishment. Every effort may be made, and indeed must be made, to resist and overcome the mastery of men over women.

The battle of the sexes described and prescribed in Genesis 3 must continue to give way to the equal partnership and cooperative relationship that is central to the creation accounts of Genesis 1 and 2. The New Testament leads the reader beyond male rule, even beyond equal partnership, to radical servanthood. Rather than husbands being assigned the rule in the home, men and women, husbands and wives, are urged to be subservient to one another out of reverence for Christ, and in imitation of Christ (Mark 10:45; Luke 22:24–27; John 13:14–17; Eph 5:21), not women subservient to men in a one-sided manner. Human ranking that is legitimised by the Bible is the ranking of parents over children (Exod 20:12; Eph 6:1–3), the model for all authority in society at large.

6. Naming confirms the man's authority over the woman (2:23; 3:20)

As the fifth pillar supporting the edifice created by those who oppose the full range of ministry positions for women in the church, it is said that the right to name another person is given only to those who have authority over that person. [14] The fact that the man names the woman (2:23; 3:20) is regarded as clear evidence of his God-given authority over her. Wenham says it means that 'she is expected to be subordinate to him' (70). By naming the animals (2:19) and the woman (2:23; 3:20), the man is said to 'establish a relation of dominion' over them (H Bietenhard, TDNT V: 253). To name a conquered city has been regarded as establishing the right of ownership, subjecting the city to the control of the conquering king or country.

Ramsey has launched a wholesale assault on such notions (*CBQ* 1988), notions that have arisen, he claims, by extension from the readily acknowledged potency of the word of God (Isa 55:10,11) and the important concept of 'performative utterance'. Ramsey doesn't wish to deny the significance of performative utterances. The words, 'On your marks, get set, go!' called out by a starter at a race meeting, do what they say; they propel the contestants around the track. One would want to include here the 'performative utterance' of God's word spoken by God's people in such contexts as blessing, or absolution, or proclamation. But it is perilous to apply this kind of potency to the words spoken by humans in general, and the naming stories of the Bible. Such words don't have the inherent quasi-magical power that has been attributed to them.

It is impossible to generalise about the function of name giving in the Old Testament. Most frequently, however, names are given which

---

14. This opinion is repeated time and time again in the overwhelming majority of Genesis commentaries. Terence Fretheim and George Ramsey are noteworthy exceptions (see references).

capture the essence of a person or object. Therefore name-giving signifies the name-giver's gift of discernment. Abigail says of her husband Nabal, 'as his name is, so is he' (1 Sam 25:25). Nabal means fool. The act of naming does not determine the attributes of the person or thing named; rather it reflects prior insight into those attributes. Thus Jacob (*ya'aqov*) received his name because he grabbed his brother Esau's heel (*'aqev*) as the twins were being born and ever after tried to cheat him by supplanting (*'aqav*) him (Gen 25:26). Presumably Adam's gift of discernment allowed him to give the animals their names based on their appearance or some typical aspect of their life-style or behaviour (2:19). And he named his partner 'Eve' (life) because he recognised her as the mother of all people living from that time onward (3:20).

Some names bear no resemblance to the person so named, but commemorate an incident or circumstance at the time of the naming (Gershom, Ex 2:22; Eliezer, Ex 18:4). Other names are given as prayers for God's help. The name Levi plays on a word for cleave, as Leah hopes his birth will make Jacob cleave to him (Gen 29:34). The name Joseph, from the verb 'to add', represents Rachel's prayer for another son (30:24). And Noah, from a verb meaning 'to rest', is his father Lamech's prophecy that his son will provide future generations with rest from their toil (5:29). Nowhere is it clearer that naming is not to be understood as the exercise of authority, or the imposition of male rule, than in Hagar's naming of God (Gen 16:13) and Mary's naming of Jesus (Luke 1:31).

At their first introduction the man names the woman 'woman' (2:23). Far from stamping his authority over her, his words are a cry of discovery. After being shown so many animals, this time he exclaims in utter joy, 'At last, God has got it right!' It is an exclamation of delight. And it is also a play on words, as the man jokes about her being called 'woman' (*'ishshah*) because she was taken out of 'man' (*'iysh*). No hint whatsoever is given that the naming is associated with male authority, or the dominion of husbands over wives.

It is readily admitted that naming is regularly done by those who are in a position of authority or control.[15] Kings and generals rename cities and villages that they have conquered (Num 32:41,42; Josh 19:47;

---

15. A clear example showing that this is not always so is Isaac's naming of two wells, Esek (contention) and Sitnah (enmity), to signify his refusal to take responsibility for them (Gen 26:20,21).

2 Sam 5:6–9), and parents have the responsibility of naming their children.[16] But parental authority and control over a city are not established by the act of naming. The name-giving is merely the sign of, or the public testimony to, the authority that is already inherent in the relationship between namer and named.

It is not hard to understand why Eve's naming has been understood as the sign and seal of Adam's authority over her. Those who come to the text already assuming the authority of husbands over wives, and men over women in the church, are quick to find in Adam's naming of the animals and his wife clear-cut support for their position. And even those who do not think of the relationship between husbands and wives in hierarchical terms have been influenced by the repeated refrain of Old Testament scholars, that naming represents and imposes authority and dominion. But name-giving does not subordinate the named to the namer. The textual support cannot be found. Instead, more often than not the evidence points to naming as a sign of the namer's ability to discern the essential features or the distinguishing behaviour of the person or object that has been named.

7. Conclusion

The two pillars drawn from Genesis 2 and the three drawn from Genesis 3 cannot bear the weight that they have been asked to bear in the church's tradition. It is vital that the reader draw the correct conclusion from the woman's derivation from the man's rib. The story has to do with the mutuality of their relationship, not the woman's secondary status. As helper, the woman overcomes male solitude and provides support for the mutual task of tilling the soil; it does not confine her to the house and restrict her to domestic duties. Nor does the writer give any hint that the woman should bear a greater portion of the blame for the fall. Furthermore, the rule of the man is the author's inspired observation regarding the state of affairs as the years unfold. And finally, far from indicating male dominion, the naming of

---

16.   It is of interest that the conferring of children's names was not the sole prerogative of the father. All but one of Jacob's children were named by Leah and Rachel (Gen 29 and 30), and he had to override Rachel's choice of the name Benoni (son of my sorrow) in order to name his last son Benjamin (Gen 35:18; see also Judg 13:1–25, where Samson is named by his anonymous mother rather than his father Manoah, even though Manoah has the lead role in the story).

the woman indicates the man's way with words ('woman' because she came out of 'man'), his delight in her creation, and his discernment of her perfect fit (2:23). And by naming her Eve, he reveals his insight into her stature as the mother of the human race (3:20).

This study raises anew the vexed question of Scripture's self-interpretation. An important rule of thumb is that unclear texts should be interpreted in the light of those that are clear. Not only are Genesis 2 and 3 the clear texts, they are also the foundational texts. The idiosyncratic use of Genesis 2 and 3 at 1 Timothy 2:13,14 serves a pastoral purpose in a problematical situation peculiar to the church at Ephesus in the New Testament period. This precludes all attempts to use the two verses in the formulation of absolute statements about what the Bible says about the role of women in the church, and the relationship of husband and wife.

This is not to say that Genesis 2 and 3 stand alone without need of further reflection in the light of the total witness of the Bible. Far from it. In terms of Scripture being its own interpreter, an initial appeal may be made to God's manner of preserving and protecting the created realm. In the universally applicable covenant with Noah, humanity is promised relief from their work and rest from the toil of their hands (Gen 5:29). This promise relates as much to male rule as it does to the pain of childbirth and the hard yakka associated with earning a living from the soil. Each is a sentence imposed following the fall; each is a description of the common plight of the human community. In light of the promise of rest and relief, each may be resisted with equal vigour. The appeal to creation is coupled with the appeal to redemption. The church confesses that Jesus Christ has taken into his own hands the cup of suffering that humans have been compelled to drink for their disobedience (Mark 14:36). He has borne in his own body the punishment humanity deserved. And having been incorporated into him by baptism and faith, Christians understand themselves to be a new creation (2 Cor 5:17). The ill effects of the fall into sin have been removed. And in the interim before faith gives way to sight, and hope to first-hand experience, the faithful are committed to the struggle to overcome the remaining vestiges of those ill effects.

References

Brueggemann, Walter, *Genesis*, Interpretation, John Knox Press, Atlanta, Georgia, 1982.

Clines, David, *What Does Eve Do to Help? And Other Readerly Questions to the Old Testament*, Sheffield Academic Press, Sheffield, 1990.

Foh, Susan, 'What is the Woman's Desire?', *Westminster Theological Journal* 37, 1974/75: 376–83.

Fretheim, Terence E, 'The book of Genesis', *The New Interpreter's Bible*, volume 1, Abingdon, Nashville, 1994, 319-674.

Friedman, Richard Elliott, *Commentary on the Torah*, Harper, San Francisco, 2001.

Gowan, Donald E, *Genesis 1–11: from Eden to Babel*, ITC, Eerdmans, Grand Rapids, 1988.

Kidner, Derek, *Genesis*, Tyndale, InterVarsity Press, Cambridge, 1967.

Luther's Works, *Lectures on Genesis*, volume 1, Concordia Publishing House, St Louis, Missouri, 1958.

Ramsey, George W, 'Is Name-Giving an Act of Domination in Genesis 2:23 and Elsewhere?' *Catholic Biblical Quarterly* 50/1, 1988: 24–35.

von Rad, Gerhard, *Genesis*, translated by John H Marks, Old Testament Library series, SCM, London, 1963.

Webb, Val, *Why We're Equal: Introducing Feminist Theology*, Chalice Press, St Louis, Missouri, 1999.

Wenham, Gordon J, *Genesis 1–15*, Word Biblical Commentary, volume 1, Word Books, Waco, Texas, 1987.

Westermann, Claus, *Genesis 1–11: a Commentary*, translated by John J Scullion, Augsburg, Minneapolis, 1984.

Disciples But Not Teachers: 1 Corinthians 14:33b–38 and 1 Timothy 2:11–15

John W Kleinig
Adelaide

In 1976 The Pontifical Biblical Commission decided that by itself the New Testament does not permit exegetes to settle the problem of the accession of women to the presbyterate. This uncertainty may explain why, in 1994, Pope John Paul II did not refer to 1 Corinthians 14:33b–35 and 1 Timothy 2:11–12 in *Ordinatio Sacerdotalis,* his *Apostolic Letter on Reserving Priestly Ordination to Men Alone,* but based his case on the precedent of Christ in choosing male apostles.

The church has not in the past shared this diffidence, since right from the beginning it justified the reservation of the apostolic ministry for men by recalling these two texts. Nor need it share this diffidence now, for they explain why the ministry of the gospel should still be reserved for men. I would therefore like to examine them closely to show how they forbid the ordination of women in the church.[1]

1.1 Corinthians 14:33b–38

Translation and structure
While commentators have often found it hard to make sense of this passage, rhetorical analysis has shown the unity of verses 33b–38 as a coherent argument (Dautzenberg: 253–73, 291-98; Hauke: 364–96). Its argument may be set out as follows:

As in all the churches[2] of the saints,

let the women remain silent in the churches,

for it is not permitted[3] for them to speak,

---

1. This essay is a reworked version of an earlier paper published in the *Lutheran Theological Journal* (Kleinig, 1995).
2. Paul uses *ekklesia* as a liturgical term both for the congregation as the assembly of the faithful and the place of assembly for worship.
3. The passive form is most likely used to indicate that God does not permit this. Aalen argues that, like the rabbis, Paul here refers to what God has forbidden in his word in contrast to what he has allowed to be done.

but let them be subordinate,[4] as the law says.
If they wish to learn something,
let them interrogate[5] their husbands at home,
  for it is shameful for a woman to speak in church.
  What, did the word of God go out from you,[6]
  or has it reached you alone?
If anyone considers that he is a prophet or a spiritual person,
let him recognise that what I write is a command of the Lord.
If, on the other hand, anybody does not acknowledge (this), he is not acknowledged (by God).[7]

Rhetorically speaking, the passage falls into two main parts. It begins with an unqualified directive for silence from women in all churches, followed by a subordinate clause explaining why they are not to speak. This reverses the previous pattern in verses 27, 28 and 29–33a of reference to 'speaking' before mentioning some restriction of it with 'silence'. Paul then treats three problems associated with this directive in three conditional sentences.

In keeping with the pattern established in verses 26–33a, the flow of the argument is determined by two third person jussives for silence and subordination in verse 34, followed by two conditional jussives about the questioning of husbands and the acknowledgment of

---

4. The active verb *tasse* means to 'place or station a person or thing in a fixed spot' (see BAGD, 1). While the passive form *hypotassomai* means 'to be placed under someone's authority' (see BAGD, 1b), its middle form signifies the willing self-location under the headship of someone in a given order. Note the play on words here in this chapter. Paul calls on women to be *subordinate* by fitting in with God's *order* for the preaching of his word and the celebration of the Lord's supper in the liturgical assembly (14:40). All members of the congregation must fit in with that divinely instituted order by practising subordination to Christ, his word, and the male teachers of his word, so that the congregation can be built up as his temple (14:26) and enjoy peace rather than *disorder* (14:33).
5. See Lockwood: 506; Thislelton: 1159f.
6. See the use of the same idiom in 1 Thess 1:8.
7. See Fee: 712. This passive form is most likely to be construed as a divine passive that refers to God's eschatological verdict. Käsemann identifies this, together with 3:17; 5:3–5 and 16:22, as an example of holy law in the New Testament (248–55).

Christ's authority in verses 35–37. This culminates in the conditional threat in verse 38 against those who reject this teaching.

Thus this passage is a coherent piece of Pauline rhetoric. It is presented in the form of regulations for the operation of the church as a liturgical community (Hauke: 267, 370–71).

The place of the passage in 1 Corinthians 14:26–40

Paul's directives on the silence of women are part of his larger discussion in 1 Corinthians 12–14 about the use of spiritual gifts in church that culminates in a discussion on the place of tongues and prophecy in public worship. More immediately, it comes as the climax of Paul's liturgical regulations in 1 Corinthians 14:26–40. In this last section Paul deals with three problems: the demand by some tongues' speakers for the right to 'speak' in tongues in the church; the demand by some prophets for the right to 'speak' their words of prophecy; and the demand by some female prophets for recognition as 'speakers in church'. Paul counters these demands for the right to speak with the demand for appropriate silence in verses 28, 30, and 34.

In keeping with this theme, the structure of 1 Corinthians 14:26-40 is as follows:

a. Introduction (26)
- General problem: the use of spiritual gifts in public worship
- General directive: the edification of the congregation

b. Speaking in tongues (27–28)
- Permissible *speaking*, if there is an interpreter
- **Silence**, with private speaking to God, if there is no interpreter

c. Speaking of prophecy (29–33a)
- Permissible *speaking* with assessment of prophecies
- **Silence**, if another prophet receives a revelation

d. Speaking of women (33b–38)
- **Silence** of women in the church
- Prohibition of *speaking* except for questioning at home

e. Conclusion (39–40)
- Encouragement of prophecy without prohibition of tongues
- Need for order in worship.

There is growing recognition among scholars that the link between 14:27–33a and 14:33b–38 is provided by Paul's requirement in 14:29 that all prophecies must be duly weighed and assessed to discover their significance and proper application (Clark: 186; Hurley: 18892;

Grudem: 250–251; Bacchiocchi: 167; Hauke: 376; Carson: 151; Witherington: 102; Thiselton: 1158). Paul does not state exactly how this is to be done. He does, however, indicate that the whole congregation ('the others') should somehow be involved in this. It probably involved a general discussion that resulted in an authoritative judgment on its sense and its application by the teachers of the congergation in the light of Christ's teaching (Matt 7:15–27; Rev 19:10), the confession of Jesus as Lord (1 Cor 12:3), and the analogy of faith (Rom 12:6).

As Johansson (57–71) has shown from Acts 20:7–12, this kind of discussion was not restricted to the weighing of prophecies; it seems also to have been associated with the homilies given by teachers in the early church. While all members could share their insights into the meaning and application of a text from the Old Testament, they could not challenge the final teaching given by the leaders of the congergation, as some women seem to have done in Corinth (1 Cor 14:35).

Paul's argument runs as follows. Speaking in tongues is allowed in worship provided that it is properly interpreted. It thereby becomes a prophecy for the congregation. Prophecies may also be given in the church provided that they are limited in number and weighed in the light of the apostolic teaching, since all prophecy is to be understood and evaluated in the light of the apostolic tradition. The reason for this is that God's Spirit does not contradict himself. So, those who hand on the apostolic tradition are finally responsible for assessing prophecy. They are the speakers in the church, those who have been appointed to teach the word of God and to ensure that it is heeded in the liturgical assembly.

The nature of the demand for silence from women

Paul's demand for the silence of women is explained in two ways. They are not permitted by God to be 'speakers' in the liturgical assembly. While the verb *lalein* is used in many different ways in the New Testament, it is never used in the sense of chattering (Barrett: 332). Here, as is often the case, it is a synonym for the teaching of God's word (eg Acts 4:1; 18:25; 1 Cor 2:6–7; 2 Cor 2:17; Heb 13:7). In addition, the silence of the women involves subordination. Remar-kably, Paul does not mention the object of their subordination. He does not refer to the general subordination of all women to all men, or the subordination of wives to husbands. Context indicates that they are to be subordinate to the male teachers of God's word and so to the word itself. Women are therefore not allowed to be speakers in the liturgical assembly, but, like all the other members of the congregation, they must be subordinate to those who have been appointed to fulfil that task. By their subordination they fit into the liturgical order that is established by the ministry of God's word in the church.

Paul quite clearly insists on relative rather than absolute silence, since he allows women to speak in tongues (1 Cor 14:5,23), prophesy (1 Cor 11:5; 14:5,23,31), and engage in liturgical prayer (1 Cor 11:5; 1 Tim 2:1–10). The kind of speaking that Paul prohibits is defined in three ways. First, a woman may not 'be a speaker in a liturgical assembly' (14:35). The unusual absolute form for 'speaking' indicates that Paul uses it as a technical term for someone authorised to speak in an official capacity (Johansson: 53,54). Since this prohibition does not apply at home it has nothing to do with the subordination of a wife to her husband.

Secondly, the forbidden speaking is associated with God's word which has come to Corinth via its apostolic emissaries from Jerusalem (14:36; see Acts 1:8; 1 Thess 2:13). We may therefore conclude that its content was the transmission and application of the apostolic teaching that had been entrusted to the leaders of the congregation, as described by Paul in 2 Timothy 2:2.

Thirdly, while this kind of 'speaking' is related to prophecy and the disputation that is connected with the weighing of prophecy in the congregation, it is nevertheless distinguished from prophecy and is more authoritative than prophecy, since it transmits the commands of Christ and requires the acquiescence of prophets (14:37–38). So when Paul forbids women to act as speakers in a liturgical assembly of the church, he excludes them from the ministry of the apostolic word.

The basis and authority for the prohibition

Paul bases his case on four sets of authority that he marshals in ascending order of importance. First, he appeals to ecumenical practice (14:33b). Some scholars claim that, since Paul uses a similar ecumenical formula in 1 Cor 4:17; 7:17 and 11:16 to conclude a section of argument, this phrase must belong to verse 33a. Yet that is most unlikely, since it is not used as a conclusion in 7:17 and it functions elsewhere to assert the catholicity of Paul's teaching (Witherington: 96; Carson: 140–41;

Thiselton: 1155).[8] Paul claims that his ruling does not just apply to the church in Corinth, but to all churches everywhere.

Secondly, he appeals to the law in the Old Testament. The absence of the far more common citation formula, 'it is written' makes it unlikely that he refers only to Genesis 3:16 or any other specific verse. Rather the use here of the summary formula: 'as the law says' (see 1 Cor 9:8), shows that Paul has in mind the whole of Genesis 2 and 3. It is best understood in the light of Paul's teaching in 1 Timothy 2:12 on the primacy of Adam, his headship as the husband of Eve,[9] and God's commission to him in Genesis 2:15–17.

Thirdly, he appeals to his hearers' sense of shame in 14:35. For Paul, shame did not just arise from failure to meet the social expectations of peers according to customary norms, as in 1 Corin-thians 11:6, but also from loss of face with God (Phil 1:20; 2 Tim 1:12), and at the failure to meet his expectations (Rom 6:21; 2 Cor 4:2; Eph 5:4,12; Col 3:8; Phil 3:19). In fact, in Ephesians 5:12, the only other place apart from 1 Corinthians 11:6 where Paul uses the formula, 'it is shameful', that formula covers what is unacceptable to God rather than what is merely socially unacceptable. In 14:35–36 the appeal to shame is closely allied with Paul's challenge to the presumptuousness of certain women prophets in questioning their teachers and in regarding themselves as either the generators or exclusive recipients of God's word.

Lastly and most significantly, Paul appeals to a specific command of the Lord in 14:37 which he has received together with other sayings of Jesus. It, like 1 Thessalonians 4:15, is not recorded in any of the gospels (see Johansson: 90–98; Hauke: 385–90; Lockwood: 511–14). As last in the list, this most weighty authority is meant to clinch the argument. When Paul speaks about the Lord's command, he most likely refers to the prohibition in verse 34. Its passive formulation denotes that it comes from God himself. Only its divine origin provides an adequate basis for his unequivocal pronouncement in 14:38 that those who reject Paul's ruling on the silence of women in the church will not be recognised by God as prophets or Spirit-filled people. Since they do not base their ministry on Christ and his word,

---

8. If it were to be taken retrospectively, it would, rather strangely, assert the catholicity of God's 'orderly' character.

9. Thus in Ephesians 5:23,32 Paul quite clearly connects the headship of a husband and the headship of Christ with the role of Adam as the primal husband.

their work will not survive the fire of God's judgment on the last day (1 Cor 3:11–14; see Hauke: 383–85; Lockwood: 514). That grave threat makes sense only in the light of Christ's prohibition of women as speakers in the church.

The appeal of Paul to such a full range of authorities discloses the gravity of the matter under discussion. If he were dealing with culturally inappropriate behaviour or disruptive chatter by women, he would have had no need to employ all these authorities. Indeed, its force would be totally disproportionate to the alleged offence, much like the use of a steamroller to squash a bull ant.[10] A simple appeal to their better senses would suffice.

To conclude: Paul's appeal to such a wide range of authorities, his mention of Christ's command, his reference to the apostolic tradition and his responsibility for it, and his threat of divine disapproval for those who reject his teaching, makes sense only if he is engaged in the defence of the divinely instituted ministry of the word.

2. 1 Timothy 2:11–15

It is generally agreed that this passage, more clearly than 1 Corinthians 14:33b-38, excludes women from the apostolic ministry of the word. Whereas that text deals with a specific situation in Corinth, Paul here gives far more general instructions to his pastoral protege Timothy about the reorganisation of the church in Ephesus.

Translation and structure
1 Timothy 2:11–15 forms a single literary unit with 2:8–10. The following translation of that unit indicates its basic structure:

> I therefore require
>> that in every place men should pray,
>>> lifting holy hands without anger and quarrelling,
>> and that women too (should pray), dressing themselves

---

10. The only other place where Paul argues in a similar fashion is in 1 Corinthians 9:3–14 where he defends his rights as an apostle. This provides an instructive parallel which, incidentally, also supports the unity of 14:33b–38. There he also works with four sets of authority: the precedent of apostolic practice (9:4–6), custom (9:7), the law (9:8–13) and the Lord's command (9:14). There he also arranges his authorities in ascending order of importance with the command of Christ as the capstone of his argument.

with modesty and chastity by means of respectable
deportment,
not by means of gold-braided hair or pearls or expensive
dress, but through good works, as is suitable for women
who profess reverence for God.
Let a woman learn in quietness[11] with entire subordination.[12]
Yet I do not permit a woman to teach
or to have authority over a man.
But she must remain in quietness;
for Adam was formed first, then Eve;
and Adam was not deceived, but the woman, being deceived,
came into transgression.
Nevertheless a woman will be saved through child bearing,
provided that she remains with chastity in faith and love and
sanctification.

Two things are worth noting in this. First, the repetition of 'chastity'
in verses 9 and 15 acts as a bracket that introduces and closes the
teaching on the participation of women in public worship. Secondly,
the repetition of 'quietness' in verses 11 and 12 creates a chiastic
construction which is highlighted by the contrast between woman and
man in verse 12a. This is how it is structured:

a. Let a woman learn in **quietness** with entire subordination.
b. Teaching, on the other hand, for a *woman* I do not permit,
b. nor having authority over a *man*,
a. but being in **quietness** (I permit).

It follows from this that Paul's main concern here is with learning
as a disciple rather than with teaching, and that 'teaching' and 'having
authority' are to be regarded as complementary activities.

The place of 1 Timothy 2:11–15 in its context
This passage is part of Paul's written pastoral 'charge' to Timothy
about his work in the church at Ephesus and the need to combat the
teachers of false doctrine there (1 Tim 1:3,18; 4:11; 5:7; 6:17). The heart

---

11. See the use of the same term in 2:2.
12. For a helpful analysis of this term, see Brunner: 24–30.

of this charge is the congregational code in 2:1-3:16.[13] This code gives instruction in how the household of God, the church of the living God, is to operate liturgically (1 Tim 3:14,15).

The congregational code covers the following matters:
a.The nature and basis of congregational prayer (2:1–7)
b.   The involvement of both sexes in congregational prayer
• Praying by men without anger and quarrelling (2:8)
• Praying by women without ostentatious dress (2:9,10)
c.The involvement of women in learning rather than in teaching (2:11–15)
d. Qualifications for leaders in public worship
• Bishops as teachers in God's household (3:1–7)
• Deacons as their assistants (3:8–13)
e.The purpose of Paul's charge (3:14–16)

The authority of Paul in 1 Timothy 2:11–15

Even though Paul uses 'I' in addressing Timothy in 1 Timothy 2:1,7,8,12, he does not give his personal opinions on congregational worship. Rather, in 2:7 he emphasises that he has been appointed by God both as an 'apostle' (see 1:1) and as a 'teacher of the faith and its truth to the gentiles'. He therefore writes about what 'must' *(dei)* be done not just in Ephesus, but in the whole church which is God's household (1 Tim 3:14,15; see Hurley: 196; Bacchiocchi: 145–48,151–52). His teaching therefore transcends the particular local problems of the church in Ephesus.[14]

The meaning of 'teaching' in the Pastoral Letters

Since 'teaching' is the key term in this text, its exact sense needs to be established before we can examine Paul's argument. Paul uses the terms for 'teaching' in a much narrower, technical sense than we do in modern English (eg 1 Cor 12:28; Eph 4:11). It usually refers to the teaching and application of God's word by Jesus and his apostles. A

---

13. See Witherington: 118. This part of Paul's letter, then, is not a household code but rather a congregational code, since he speaks about conduct in the church as God's household (contra Towner: 210).

14. The ecumenical extent of his charge is also evident from his instruction in 2:11 about prayer 'in every place' of worship (see Mal 1:11; Cor 1:2; 2 Cor 2:14; 1 Thess 1:8; 2 Thess 3:16).

teacher hands on the apostolic tradition and uses it to build up the church as a liturgical community.

As the teacher of the gentiles (1 Tim 2:7), the apostle Paul is also a teacher of the gospel (2 Tim 1:11) which God has entrusted to him (1 Tim 1:11). He has been Timothy's teacher (1 Tim 1:2; 2 Tim 2:2) and has passed on to him what he himself has received from Christ (2 Tim 1:13,14). Paul therefore urges Timothy to teach what he has received from him (1 Tim 4:11; 6:2) and to live a life consistent with that teaching (1 Tim 4:16). Timothy is to use the Old Testament (2 Tim 3:16) and the words of Jesus (1 Tim 4:6; 6:3) in his teaching which is usually associated with the public reading of the Scriptures (1 Tim 4:13) and the preaching of the word to the congregation (2 Tim 4:2). By teaching he convinces and encourages his hearers (2 Tim 4:2); he rebukes and corrects those who teach what is contrary to the apostolic tradition (1 Tim 1:3). So Timothy is required to hand on to other faithful men what he has been taught by Paul, and to appoint them as teachers in the church (2 Tim 2:2).

Paul uses a number of terms to describe the role of the teachers in the church. As 'bishops' they supervise the worship and life of the congregation (1 Tim 3:2). As 'elders' they arrange the worship of the congregation and manage its operation (1 Tim 5:17). As 'servants' of the risen Lord they represent him in their teaching and work with him (2 Tim 2:24). Their basic qualification is that they are teachable and skilled in teaching (1 Tim 3:2; 2 Tim 2:24). They teach God's word in the church (1 Tim 5:17); they use the healing doctrine of Christ to encourage the faithful and to refute those who contradict it (Tit 1:9).

So then, for Paul a teacher is a minister of God's word, a pastor who has been authorised to teach what the apostles taught.

The argument of 1 Timothy 2:11–15

Paul makes it quite clear that, unlike Jewish women who did not join in the public prayers of the synagogue and were not allowed to be students of the rabbis, Christian women were expected to join in the intercession of the church for the world and to 'learn' God's word as disciples of Jesus Christ. In fact, he commands them to be disciples, students who learn God's word. The unusual absolute form of this verb suggests that this command has to do with being disciples rather than with learning a particular lesson. Like all the men, they too are recipients of the apostolic tradition (2 Tim 3:14). As disciples they are to pray and do good works. These activities, rather than teaching, are the marks of their discipleship.

Their proper disposition as disciples is characterised by two terms. First, they are to learn in quietness. This describes their attitude to God's word, their state of being as disciples. Such quietness involves stillness and harmony, receptivity and teachability, respectful listening and readiness to receive direction (see Acts 11:18; 21:14; 22:2; 1 Thess 4:11; 2 Thess 3:12; 1 Tim 2:2). It is the mark of a wise learner, a sage who never ceases to be student. Secondly, women are to be in a state of entire subordination. As in 1 Corinthians 14:34, Paul does not mention the object of their subordination. Since it is linked with being a disciple, it refers to Christ's word and to those who teach that word rather than to men in general (Moo: 183).

Even though women must be disciples, they are not permitted to teach in the liturgical assembly. The use of *de* introduces a contrast between learning which is commanded and teaching which is forbidden (Bacchiocchi: 149; Moo: 184). In other words, 2:12 explains the concept of subordination in negative terms. The responsibility for teaching in public worship is associated with the 'exercise of authority' over a man.[15] The sense of 'a man' is not immediately clear. While it could be men in general or a husband, it most obviously refers to the male teacher(s) of the congregation. The relationship between teaching and exercising authority can be taken in three ways. Paul could be prohibiting two separate activities or two identical activities or, most likely, from the syntax, two similar activities (Köstenberger). Whatever the case, it is clear that Paul does not allow women to be teachers in the church.

Paul bases the subordination of women to their male teachers on God's will as revealed in the priority of Adam's creation. God appointed him as the teacher of his wife and his family by giving him his original command and promise (Gen 2:16,17). The priority of Adam established his God-given responsibility to be the head of the human family; it also established firstborn males as the heads of every Israelite family. As such they were the teachers of their families. In worship they represented their families before God. This role of Adam as the liturgical head of the human family was fulfilled by Christ (see Col 1:15–23); it is now exercised by him through the male teachers in the church.

---

15. For this translation of *authentein*, see Panning, Knight, and Köstenberger.

While Paul's mention of Adam's priority over Eve establishes the position of male teachers in the congregation, his subsequent reference to Eve's deception is a warning against the refusal of some women in Ephesus to remain students of God's word. The point of comparison is between Eve as an insubordinate student of God's word and all Christian women as receptive disciples. Thus Paul does not assert that women should be excluded from the ministry of the word because they are more responsible for the fall than Adam, or because they are somehow more susceptible to deception by Satan than men. That is obviously not so. Rather, he warns that Christian women should not become teachers like Eve, but remain disciples of Christ, subordinate to him and his word and to those who teach that word.

So, while Paul teaches the full involvement of all women in the public worship of the church as intercessors and disciples, he does not allow them to be teachers in the church.

3. Conclusion

The exalted Lord Jesus has appointed ministers of the gospel to convey his gifts to the faithful in the church. He has chosen to do so by calling male apostles and male teachers of his word. But he has not authorised any women to perform this ministry. Paul, in fact, claims that Christ has forbidden women to be teachers in the assembly of the saints. Christ has not given them the task of giving his word and his sacraments to the people of God. So, since he has not given it to them, they cannot exercise this ministry without usurping that office in violation of Christ's command.

References

Aalen, S, 'A Rabbinical Formula in 1 Corinthians 14:34', in FL Cross, *Studia Evangelica* 11/1, Akademie-verlag, Berlin, 1964, 513–25.

Bacchiocchi, Samuele. *Women in the Church. A Biblical Study on the Role of Women in the Church,* Biblical Perspectives 7, Berrien Springs, 1987.

Barrett, CK, *A Commentary on the First Epistle to the Corinthians,* Black: London, 2d edition, 19710.

Brunner, Peter, *The Ministry and the Ministry of Women,* Concordia Publishing House: Saint Louis, 1971.

Carson, DA, '"Silent in the Churches": On the Role of Women in 1 Corinthians 14:33b–36', in J Piper and W Grudem, *Recovering Biblical Manhood and Womanhood,* Crossway Books: Wheaton, 1991, 140–53.

Clark, Stephen. *Man and Woman in Christ*, Servant Publications: Ann Arbor, 1980.

Dautzenberg, Gerhard, *Urchristliche Prophetie. Ihre Forschung, ihre Voraussetzungen im Judentum und ihre Struktur im ersten Korintherbrief*, BWANT 104, Kohlhammer: Stuttgart, 1975.

Fee, Gordon, *The First Epistle to the Corinthians*, Eerdmans: Grand Rapids, 1987.

Grudem, Wayne, *The Gift of Prophecy in 1 Corinthians*, University Press of America: Washington DC, 1982.

Hauke, Manfred, *Women in the Priesthood. A Systematic Analysis in the Light of the Order of Creation and Redemption*, Ignatius Press: San Francisco, 1988.

Hurley, James B, *Man and Woman in Biblical Perspective. A Study in Role Relationships and Authority*, Intervarsity Press: Leicester, 1981.

Johansson, Nils, *Women and the Church's Ministry An Exegetical Study of 1 Corinthians 11–14*, St Barnabas: Ottawa, 1972.

Käsemann, E, 'Sentences of Holy Law in the NT', in *NT Questions of Today*, SCM: London, 66–81.

Kleinig, John W, 'Scripture, and the Exclusion of Women from the Pastorate (I)', *Lutheran Theological Journal* 29/2 (1995): 74–81, and 'Scripture, and the Exclusion Of Women from the Pastorate (II)', *Lutheran Theological Journal* 29/3 (1995): 123–29.

Knight, George. '*Authentein* in Reference to Women in 1 Timothy 2:12', *New Testament Studies* 30 (1984): 143–157.

Köstenberger, Andreas J, 'Syntactical Background Studies to 1 Timothy 2:12 in the New Testament and Extrabiblical Greek Literature', in Stanley E Porter and DA Carson, *Discourse Analysis and Other Topics in Biblical Greek*, Sheffield Academic Press: Sheffield, 1995, 156–179.

Lockwood, Gregory J, *1 Corinthians*, Concordia Commentary, Concordia Publishing House: Saint Louis, 2000.

Moo, Douglas. 'What Does It Mean Not To Teach or Have Authority Over Men?, 1 Timothy 2:11–15', in J Piper and W Grudem, *Recovering Biblical Manhood and Womanhood*, Crossway Books: Wheaton, 1991, 179–93.

Panning. Armin J, '*Authentein*—A Word Study', *Wisconsin Lutheran Quarterly* 78 (1981): 185–191.

Pope John Paul II. *Ordinatio Sacerdotalis. Apostolic Letter on Reserving Priestly Ordination to Men Alone*, at: http://www.cin.org /users/ james/files/w-ordination.htm, 1994-May-22.

Thiselton, Anthony C, *The First Epistle to the Corinthians*, The New International Greek Testament Commentary, Eerdmans: Grand Rapids, Michigan, and Paternoster Press: Carlisle, 2000.

Towner, Philip H, *The Goal of Our Instruction. The Structure of Theology and Ethics in the Pastoral Epistles*, JSOT Supplement 34, JSOT Press: Sheffield, 1989.

Witherington, Ben. *Women in the Earliest Churches*, Cambridge University Press: Cambridge, 1988.

New Wine in New Skins? — The Ordination of Women and the Anglican Church of Australia

Muriel Porter
Melbourne

The late Monica Furlong, the revered English matriarch of the contemporary struggle for women's ordination in the Anglican Church, was quite clear that arguments offered against women in ministry were not really important in themselves. What was important was what they hid, she maintained. Underneath the rhetoric, men and women were very frightened of each other and of what the debate about the ordination of women would reveal, she said in an interview during an Australian visit in 1984. The debate about women was just the 'tip of the iceberg'; the real issue confronting the Church was sexuality in general, she said.[1]

More than twenty years later, few commentators or theologians have explored the issue as Ms Furlong portrayed it, at least in Australia. The many synodical and other debates on women's ordination across those years, including the debate on women bishops at the 2004 General Synod, have been curiously detached and cerebral, despite the passionate energy that has surrounded them. This is true of the arguments used by both sides. They have, almost invariably, coalesced around a few standard, well-worn areas: biblical authority, the tradition of the Church, and to a lesser extent, the experience of women in ministry, from both perspectives—Scripture, tradition and reason, as we might put it, the 'three-fold cord not easily broken' that the sixteenth century divine Richard Hooker discerned at the heart of Anglican polity.

Any perceptive church historian, however, would affirm that the arguments offered in public theological debates, while they may seem to be about theology, are essentially political. They are the arguments

---

1. Author interview with Monica Furlong in Melbourne, May 1984. Published in *Church Scene*, 25 May 1984.

designed to win over opponents or shore up supporters, sometimes by sheer force of logic, sometimes by gentle persuasion, and other times perhaps by public ridicule. Astute church politicians, like their secular counterparts, organise their debating weaponry only after careful assessment of who is to be persuaded (and who it is not worth trying to persuade), and what kind of argument will be most likely to win over their targets. They will know there is little to be gained, and perhaps much to be lost, in revealing the real reasons that have persuaded them to their position. Perhaps, as Ms Furlong suggested, they might not even be consciously aware of their inner compulsions on the matter, particularly if they lie close to the heart.

The long-running debate about clergy marriage in the English Reformation is an interesting case in point.[2] The proponents of clerical marriage argued mainly from the basis of Scripture, most often refuting the traditional use of 1 Corinthians 7 (the second half of the first verse of which states ominously: 'it is well for a man not to touch a woman' NRSV) to support priestly celibacy. The traditionalists used this half-verse (and other proof texts) to support the over-riding imperative of cultic purity, that is, that the priest at the altar handling the body and blood of Christ must be undefiled, principally by abstaining from intimate contact with women. The reformers seized on a later verse (verse 9) in that same chapter—'It is better to marry than to be aflame with passion' (the reformers used the more colourful old turn of phrase, 'it is better to marry than to burn')—to justify their advocacy of optional clerical marriage. Celibacy was certainly the preferred, indeed only, option for those few clergy with the spiritual 'charism' required to live chaste lives, claimed the reformers, who clearly harboured residual cultic purity concerns. Marriage however was necessary for the vast majority of priests without the charism, so that their wholesome married lives could be 'living sermons' for the laity. The common scandal of too many supposedly celibate clergy not living chaste lives at all was all the proof they needed to offer for that debating point! It is telling that the reformers tended to concentrate on reworking these well-worn debates rather than focussing primarily on the strong, unambiguous biblical warrant for married clergy to be

---

2.   See Muriel Porter, 'The Defence of the Marriage of Priests in the English Reformation', University of Melbourne PhD thesis, 1988; also Muriel Porter, *Sex, Marriage and the Church: Patterns of Change* (Melbourne: Dove, 1996).

found in 1 Timothy 3:2—'A bishop must be . . . married only once'—and its companion verse, Titus 1:6.

The reformers also argued from tradition, on the basis that clergy had until the twelfth century been allowed to be married. Their opponents had an answer from tradition though, maintaining that Jesus himself and his apostles (conveniently ignoring the biblical reference to Peter's mother-in-law) were not married, thus setting the standard for their representatives for all time.

But behind these intellectual arguments can be discerned very different motivations. For the reformers, a married priesthood demolished any supposed ontological distinction between clergy and people in line with their Protestant insight that faith was a matter between God and the individual without need of an intermediary priest. Clergy were essentially the same as laymen in the eyes of God. Secondly, as the reformers personally experienced marriage, even if they had married initially to demonstrate their commitment to their Protestant principles rather than out of personal preference, they began to internalise their argument that marriage was indeed an 'honourable estate' for all men. However, they seem to have been loath to argue out of that experience, presumably lacking confidence to claim publicly that marriage, and sexual activity within marriage, was as holy a vocation as celibacy. This was a new theological insight that would not develop fully until the third and fourth generations of married theologians.

On the other side, behind the traditional cultic purity arguments, historians have identified the real reason for the twelfth century change in church law that enforced clerical celibacy as being the creation of an internationalised papal church government. This required a loyal and flexible cohort of clergy undistracted by the claims of family, kinship and property, a reason that at least one commentator has claimed still holds true today.[3]

So what really lies behind the arguments regularly advanced for and against the ordination of women in the Anglican Church? What motivations do the arguments hide? Was Monica Furlong right in her

---

3. Former Australian priest Paul Collins has written: 'Underlying Rome's insistence on celibacy is the question of power. The celibate man is the Church's man with no other focus to his life except the Church.' *Mixed Blessings: John Paul II and the Church of the Eighties—the Crisis in World Catholicism and the Australian Church* (Melbourne: Penguin, 1986), 77.

assessment? With the debate not yet over in this country and with perhaps another decade or more still to run, no definitive answers are yet possible. Those of us deeply committed to the issue and immersed in it at many levels are certainly not able to offer a dispassionate assessment. But there are some clues that suggest the public debate masks the real motivations.

On the side of the supporters of the ordination of women, two theologians—nearly three decades apart—have offered an important but little explored perspective. In 1976, when the debate about women priests in Australia was just warming up, Bishop Max Thomas, then Bishop of Wangaratta and a member of the General Synod Doctrine Commission, argued that the only real theological point at issue concerned God's call. The Church's main task, he said, was to decide whether God was calling women to the priesthood.[4] 'The Church has always had various ways of determining this question of vocation when men seek ordination,' he explained. The Church should simply have tested the vocations of the women in the same way. 'If the answer was "yes, God is calling this person to priesthood", then all the rest would have been a clearing of the ground.'[5]

On a visit to Melbourne in early 2005, an English woman priest and theologian made the same point in relation to women bishops. Canon Dr Jane Shaw, Dean of Divinity at New College, University of Oxford, identified God's 'call' and 'gifts' as the two key questions for the ongoing debate about women bishops. God's call to the episcopate was regardless of gender, and the Church's role was to affirm that call, she said. No one decided to be a deacon, priest or bishop: 'They are called by the Holy Spirit'. Similarly, God gave people, male or female, the gifts to be bishops. It was a serious matter when the Church failed to hear or respond to the call of God, or to recognise the gifts God had given, she argued.[6]

Both Bishop Thomas and Dr Shaw, without denying the possibility that women had also been called to ordained ministry in earlier times, have proposed that God is doing something new in these latter days. *God* is calling women into the ordained ministry, and the Church's responsibility is to discern the nature of God's activity in the women

---

4. *Sun News-Pictorial*, 2 October 1976.
5. Author interview, 15 April 1988.
6. Canon Dr Jane Shaw, public lecture, Trinity College Theological School, Melbourne, 11 March 2005.

who attest to a call, using the same methods it employs when men present for ordination. The Church's primary response should not be to ignore the work of God by indulging in theological argument! However, as Bishop Thomas pointed out years ago, the Church, in its public discourse, has consistently refused to concentrate on this one central theological question.[7]

Few other advocates of women's ministry have argued that this is the central question. This is actually quite surprising because, in private conversation, many supporters readily acknowledge that their commitment to the cause of women's ordination was first sparked by the realisation that God was calling individual women, perhaps even themselves, to ordination. Certainly many male clerical supporters could date their conversion to the cause to an encounter with a woman parishioner who told them of her call. When it came to public debate, however, these experiences have largely remained private.

Have the proponents of women's ordination allowed themselves to be sidetracked into secondary questions? Bishop Thomas has suggested as much. From the beginning of the debate, the issue was posed in negative terms, he has reminded us. Theologians looked for theological objections to women clergy, rather than affirmations.[8] In these terms, if women priests proved acceptable, they would be an 'optional extra' rather than an essential component of contemporary Christian ministry. Hardly a faithful ecclesial response to God's 'new thing'! If advocates had handled the question differently, positively, from the beginning, there would have been little doubt that this issue was nothing less than a case of new wine in new wineskins.

The underlying implications are profound. If women can and are being called by God to the three-fold order of Christian ministry, what does that say about women? (The corollary is also true; I will turn to that aspect below.) In hindsight, the proponents of women's ordination may have too often sold women short for transitory, political reasons, or even because they were actually nervous of claiming too much, like the first married reformers. It is much easier, much less complicated, and much less confronting to behave as if the change you seek would be essentially secondary. We assured our opponents (and perhaps ourselves?) that we were not seeking to change the Church itself, or its orders; no, we just wanted to add women into the existing structures.

---

7.   Author interview, 15 April 1988.
8.   Author interview, 15 April 1988.

Fundamentally, we argued from the negative perspective—there was no reason, neither theological nor biblical nor constitutional, *not* to ordain women. Only occasionally did we argue from a truly affirmative position that insisted that without women, Anglican orders and the Anglican Church itself were less than God was calling them to be.

Ironically, some early opponents understood the full scope of the issue better than the proponents. They understood only too well why they thought women could not be priests, when they spoke dismissively of 'priestesses', when they referred to the Movement for the Ordination of Women as the Movement for the Ordination of Witches, when they laughed at the prospect of pregnant women in chasubles or menstruating women celebrating Holy Communion. The disparagement of women *per se* that was part and parcel of the debate, particularly in the 1980s, was telling.[9] For these opponents, the aim of ordaining women was a dark secular feminist plot to destroy the church; its protagonists were pagan, unfeminine, likely to be lesbians, unnatural, egocentric, and eccentric. It was obviously disturbing to them at a deep level. Perhaps the most pointed comment of all was that made by a Sydney layman in a paper presented in 1987: 'Is it possible that the Church now thinks so little of Holy Orders that it is prepared to open them to women?'[10]

Archbishop Peter Carnley of Perth, speaking at the 1987 General Synod, described opposition to women clergy as as much 'psycho-spiritual' as theological, and certainly there was truth in his claim. But I would argue that the opposition goes far deeper than the individual, subconscious misogyny to which he was referring. Underneath was and is a largely unexamined corporate assumption, grounded in longstanding Church cultural patterns and behaviour, that women are inferior to men. And not just inferior in physical and intellectual areas, but more importantly, in moral and spiritual arenas. More, women have been feared because of their sexuality, their female otherness. The prospect of allowing them to be priests unleashed the hidden demon of theological misogyny with a ferocity that surprised many in the latter decades of the twentieth century. We tried not to engage in debate

---

9. The letters column in *Church Scene* in June and July, 1986, offer potent examples of this material.

10. GC Lindsay, 'Authority in the church: an attempt at analysis', Sydney, 24 August 1987. Quoted in Muriel Porter, *Women in the Church: The Great Ordination Debate in Australia* (Melbourne: Penguin, 1989) 176.

along these lines, mainly because we did not want to dignify it with a serious response. In hindsight, I suspect we should have responded to that disturbing revelation by developing and promoting a cohesive and comprehensive theology of sexual equality. And by failing to respond, we effectively colluded with an ancient and pervasive wrong.

The other side has not been so reticent. In recent years, the opponents of women's ordination have been tireless in re-establishing a theology of female subordination. While supporters readily dismissed as quaint the 'male headship' argument (which insists that the New Testament requires the head of the family and of the congregation to be male), conservative theologians were busy reshaping and representing it. In the latter years of the twentieth centuries, theologians from both North America and Sydney have embedded the headship claim in the doctrine of the Trinity, no less. This is a complex argument which cannot be treated adequately here but the conservative revision can be summarised as claiming that Christ the Son is eternally subordinated in role or function to God the Father. God the Father, it is claimed, has eternal 'headship' over the Son, modelling the 'headship' of men over women while still allowing 'equality in being/essence/nature/dignity'.[11] This supposed hierarchical ordering within the Trinity is used to justify the subordination of women in the two areas over which the Church has some continuing influence—leadership in the Church, and male-female relationships within marriage. The 'new' doctrine has been called 'subordinationism'.

Subordinationism has been strongly refuted by theologians and biblical scholars, and in particular by Melbourne priest Dr Kevin Giles, himself an Evangelical. Dr Giles has written at length on this subject[12] but two key points of his argument are relevant here. First, this conservative Evangelical interpretation of the Trinity is an interpretation developed to justify the permanent subordination of women. It is 'novel and dangerous', he claims, and wrong because a Christ differentiated from the Father in function and authority and possibly being, is in direct contradiction to the catholic faith defined by the Nicene and Athanasian creeds. Second, the interpretation is a

---

11. Kevin Giles, *The Trinity and Subordinationism: The Doctrine of God and the Contemporary Gender Debate* (Downers Grove, Illinois: IVP, 2002) 23.

12. Kevin Giles, *The Trinity and Subordinationism, passim.*

significant break with Christian historical tradition, in that for nineteen centuries, orthodox exegetes and theologians understood the Bible as teaching that women were subordinate and inferior to men and so to be excluded from leadership in *both society and the Church.* Women's exclusion from leadership in Church and marriage was of a piece with their exclusion from public life in all forms, and from exercising any authority over men. Hence women were barred from the right to vote, for example, and once married, had no legal rights at all over their property or even their children. To be consistent and to keep faith with the traditional Christian position, those who claim biblical warrant for the subordination of women in home and Church should also seek their barring from all spheres of public life where they would exercise authority over men.

The commitment to barring women from ordained ministry, then, has resulted in a far-reaching revision of fundamental Christian theology and a reinterpretation of Christian tradition. The doctrine of the Trinity has been substantially reworked, inevitably involving doctrines concerned with the nature of Christ and the salvation of humankind, as well as the relationship between women and men. By these lights, misogyny has been restated as a divine imperative, and the outrageous claims made against women who claimed they were being called to ordination, as outlined above, have tacitly been justified. The proponents of subordinationism do not use the offensive terminology of the 1980s opposition to women priests, but their theory nevertheless supports the claim that women who sought ordination *were* behaving in unnatural, unfeminine, pagan, egocentric and eccentric ways; more, they were defying God, as were their supporters. Further arguments from Scripture, tradition and reason were so much wasted breath. The big question is: does the same fear of the female, as evidenced in the disparaging assertions of the 1980s, really underlie these sophisticated, seemingly rational arguments as well?

It is interesting that the full development of this doctrinal justification for women's subordination took some thirty years, if we take the 1968 Lambeth Conference resolution commending study of women's ordination as our starting point. It was there in summary form, however, in the first report on the subject by the Australian General Synod Commission on Doctrine in 1973. Though a two-thirds majority of the theologians on the Commission supported the ordination of women to all three orders, the minority claimed that 'nature, the law, the commandment of the Lord and apostolic teaching'

all corroborated the permanence of St Paul's teaching in 1 Corinthians
14:34: 'Let your women keep silence in the churches . . . they are
commanded to be under obedience' (Authorised Version).[13] The
inclusion of 'nature' in that list is telling.

The Doctrine Commission's majority support for women clergy
was based on the opposite understanding: women enjoyed full
spiritual equality with men, were created in the image of God as men
were, and had the same authority over creation. Christ had restored
the original order of creation, and with it women's equality.[14] This
argument reflects the underlying reason why most supporters of
women's ordination have been prepared to accept the possibility that
God calls women as well as men to holy orders: we accept as a given
the full equality of women; more, we believe it is God-given. However,
to support our primary case, we have not seriously engaged in the
same in-depth exegesis of the doctrines of God and humanity as our
opponents have, except in brief refutation. In this last and crucial stage
of the argument in the Anglican Church of Australia, this has proved
to be a serious omission. The arguments of those opposing women
bishops at the 2004 General Synod were centred in the claim that
women bishops would be an ungodly innovation borne of secular
feminism rather than obedience to God. I suspect we did not answer
that central issue as strenuously as it required.

At the time of writing, the most recent official count of the number
of Anglican women clergy in Australia indicated there were about 500
female deacons and priests, constituting about one sixth of the total. In
some major dioceses, such as Melbourne and Brisbane, they are about
one fifth. Women clergy are offering significant, creative and sensitive
ministry at many levels, but not yet in real leadership because there are
no women bishops. There is still no legislation to provide for their
entry into this key level of church government, thanks largely to the
opposition marshalled by Sydney Diocese at the 2004 General Synod
on the grounds of subordinationism. The Anglican Church, then,
remains a male-dominated church, though two thirds of its membership is female. Without women in leadership, the Church is, in secular
terms, a discriminatory, unbalanced workplace. In spiritual terms, if
God *is* calling women into all three holy orders, it is not only deprived

---

13.   Report of the Commission on Doctrine to the fourth General Synod,
      1973, in *General Synod Church of England in Australia 1973*, 334ff.
14.   *Ibid.*

of the fullness of Christian ministry and experience, but also disobedient.

At the same time as the debate over women's ordination has been proceeding in the Anglican Church in this country and elsewhere, an international debate over homosexuality has also been ignited. There is not the space here to discuss this issue, but it is important to indicate that there are close parallels between the two. Both of them, ironically, are linked to the development of safe, reliable and acceptable artificial contraceptives, in particular 'the pill', which was released onto the world market in 1961. The pill gave Western women complete control over their fertility for the first time in history, enabling women to have careers as well as families, and a new-found confidence and freedom in their female bodiliness and sexuality. This offered women the capacity to enjoy sexual activity without fear of unwanted pregnancy. Sexual pleasure for its own sake, quite divorced from procreation, began to be respectable, as the 1958 Lambeth Conference had heralded in its landmark acceptance of contraception.[15]

This new female freedom obviously made ordination a real possibility for women, but more importantly, it gave devout women the confidence to hear, and respond to, the call of God. We should not underestimate the importance of a holistic understanding of femaleness in this regard. If you have no control over your fertility and therefore no realistic autonomy in your life, it is difficult to believe,

---

15. The committee that prepared the 1958 Lambeth resolution on contraception, produced a thoughtful report which examined carefully the arguments about the purposes of marriage. While it acknowledged the purpose of procreation, it gave equal weight to sexual union for relational reasons: 'Husbands and wives owe to each other and to the depth and stability of their families the duty to express, in sexual intercourse, the love which they bear and mean to bear to each other. Sexual intercourse is not by any means the only language of earthly love, but it is, in its full and right use, the most intimate and the most revealing; it has the depth of communication signified by the Biblical word so often used for it, 'knowledge'; it is a giving and receiving in the unity of two free spirits which is in itself good (within the marriage bond) and mediates good to those who share it. Therefore it is utterly wrong to urge that, unless children are specifically desired, sexual intercourse is of the nature of sin. It is also wrong to say that such intercourse ought not to be engaged in except with the willing intention to procreate children.' *The Lambeth Conference 1958* (London: SPCK 1958), 147.

deep down, in your full spiritual equality. No wonder it was almost exclusively unmarried women—nuns and spinster—in earlier generations who constituted the few female representatives among the saints, doctors and luminaries of the Church.

This radical change in the understanding of human sexuality also affected homosexual people. The abolition of criminal sanctions against consenting, private adult homosexual activity from the 1970s on, confirmed a new bodily freedom for homosexuals. The call for gay ordination (and the blessing of same-sex unions) is the inevitable outworking of a dynamic similar to that which has impacted the lives of women since the 1960s, and is intimately connected with the extension of ordination to women. A common thread in opposition to both issues is fear of the feminine and the unrestrained sexuality it represents. As Monica Furlong said, the ordination of women is but the tip of the iceberg; the real issue is sexuality, an area the Church has traditionally found confronting.

In the light of this, it is not surprising that the dramatic threats of schism that have destabilised the Anglican Church in recent decades, both in Australia and internationally, have been in response either to the ordination of women or of gay people. Claims of impaired communion, demands for alternative episcopal oversight or non-geographic dioceses, have been made in response to these twin issues, which once might have been more realistically identified as 'second order' matters. Schism might be understandable as a response to disputes over credal doctrines, such as the divinity/humanity of Christ, or his resurrection or virgin birth. Instead, sexuality—female or gay —has become the line in the sand for Christian orthodoxy. The claim that these recent disputes are at heart a debate over the authority of Scripture does not hold weight, given that respectable Bible scholars hold divergent interpretations of the key texts in these areas. The authority of Scripture could have been far more powerfully evoked in the 1970s/1980s debate over divorce in the Anglican Communion. Divorce was a matter on which our Lord was clearly prescriptive, and on which there have also been divergent views, though without the same eruption of emotional name-calling.[16] Divorce, though it is

---

16.   See Muriel Porter, 'Scripture and the breaking of communion; an historical overview' in Scott Cowdell and Muriel Porter, editors, *Lost in Translation? Anglicans, Controversy and the Bible: Perspectives from the Doctrine Commission of the Anglican Church of Australia* (Melbourne: Desbooks, 2004), 139–155.

tangentially concerned with issues of human sexuality and female autonomy, does not impact sexuality directly. It is not concerned with the central issue of male/female spiritual equality in the same way.

If my thesis is correct, the 2004 General Synod debate on women bishops did not deal with the real issues behind the issue, any more than previous debates on the subject. Supporters of the cause did not fully engage the real question of female subordination, assuming that argument had been put to bed when women priests were won in 1992. Nor, more seriously, did they fully and confidently assert, in the Church's political arena, their profound belief in God's new call to women, in these days at least, into all the ministries of the Church. It is time that they did.

The Ordination of Women and Political Repentance

Peter G Bolt
Sydney

The debates concerning the ordination of women have been conducted for long enough to enable some perspective to be gained from hindsight. A spectrum of positions taken with respect to the ordination of women has emerged—from full endorsement, through partial endorsement, to total rejection.

The contributors to this issue of *Interface* have been selected to represent a variety of positions. We have been asked by the editors, to reflect, from within our own situation, on 'the present struggles with respect to the ordination of women'. I write as an Anglican evangelical, who resides in, and plays an active part in the affairs of, Sydney Diocese, where the ordination of women to the priesthood has been consistently and thoughtfully rejected on biblical and theological grounds. From this perspective, the 'struggle' with respect to this issue, arises from the desire to continue to hold this position as the appropriate response to God's word, in the belief that it is the best possible course for all concerned. When crafted in this form, the struggle necessarily entails a desire for those who have permitted the ordination of women to adopt a different position and so to 'turn back the clock'. That is, the struggle is one of continued commitment to persuasion, which—to introduce the particular concern of this paper—will include a call for repentance.

1. The place of politics in denominational life

1.1 Politics and Belief

Politics concerns how groups of people act together in an organised way. Inevitably, therefore, there is a political side to church life and denominational associations. Although there are those who speak as if politics is the only reality, especially within Sydney Anglicanism,[1] this is a view 'from the outside',[2] rather than a serious attempt to grapple 'from within' with the complex realities that pertain as Christians seek to act in an organised way. For most of the twentieth century, those studying and speaking of organised group behaviour operated from assumptions that tended to minimise the role played by the beliefs of the membership. Thankfully, some sociologists of religion have begun to challenge this older, entrenched sociological assumption, arguing that, when it comes to Christianity, belief cannot be marginalised or minimised. Rodney Stark[3] has argued that, from a sociological point of view, early Christianity grew rapidly as a direct result of its beliefs. So, for example, it was a positive belief in the afterlife that enabled Christians to care for the sick, in extraordinary ways when compared to the treatment usually given them. Christian belief about the value of human life led to Christians refusing such things as abortion and infanticide, as well as to their care of the exposed infants of the pagans, and the value and importance of women was another remarkable Christian belief. It was beliefs such as these that contributed to the growth of the movement, from a sociological point of view. Whatever may be true of other groups, the 'politics' of *this* group cannot be extracted from larger complexities, and, in particular, from what Christians believe.

---

1.   See, perhaps, Chris McGillion, *The Chosen Ones: the Politics of Salvation in the Anglican Church* (Sydney: Allen & Unwin, 2005). In his book, *Reflections in Glass. Trends and tensions in the contemporary Anglican Church* (Sydney: HarperCollins [Aust], 2004), Archbishop Peter Carnley provides another view of Sydney Anglicanism from the outside, recognising that there is more to the equation simply than politics.

2.   Older studies in the humanities tended to give 'etic' descriptions of the people under study ('from the outside'), rather than 'emic' descriptions arising from listening to what the subjects say about themselves. Thankfully, this older imperialistic attitude is now being questioned in some quarters; KL Pike, 'Etic and Emic Standpoints for the Description of Behavior', in AG Smith (editor), *Communication in Culture. Reading in the Codes of Human Interaction* (New York: Holt, Rinehart, Winston, 1966), 152–163.

3.   Rodney Stark, *The Rise of Christianity. How the Obscure, Marginal Jesus Movement Became the Dominant Religious Force in the Western World in a Few Centuries* (San Francisco: HarperCollins, 1997 [Princeton: 1996]).

There are, of course, many beliefs that are of specific relevance to the ordination of women debate. In addition to these, Christian 'politicians' should also be controlled by core Christian beliefs of a more general nature. So, for example, it almost goes without saying, that the basic dominical command to the love of God and the love of one's neighbour (Mark 12:28–34) ought to temper the behaviour and speech of the parties of any debate, especially towards those deemed their 'opponents'.

This paper seeks to reflect upon yet another core Christian belief, namely, that of repentance. The appeal for repentance has surfaced in the discussions of the last thirty or so years. Where the love command has been breached, or where attitudes or behaviours have been wrong, it is understandable that the appeal for repentance follows hard after. This article addresses a more particular question. How should the New Testament's teaching on the importance and necessity of repentance, help to inform a reflection upon the struggles in regard to the ordination of women, when this reflection takes place within a situation that maintains 'a conservative position'?

1.2 Politics and the rhetoric of change

Just as surely as Christian belief lies behind Christian behaviour, so too, political beliefs lie behind political behaviour. In the history of the early years of the British in New South Wales, the time under Governor Richard Bourke (December 1831–December 1837) saw the emergence of a new flavour in the political life of the colony. Bourke has been described as 'the champion of liberalism'.[4] Political liberalism was the mood that characterised British political and intellectual life in the 1830s, and, when transferred to an Australia engaged in constitutional debate throughout the 1830s to 1850s, its impact was felt in such themes as 'the development of free market forces, abolition of privilege, philanthropy (real, if shallow), [and] belief that men of the past were usually wrong or corrupt whereas present ideals were pure'.[5]

Behind this last-mentioned concern of political liberalism, of course, lies a good dose of the Enlightenment belief in 'inevitable progress'.

---

4.   Michael Roe, '1830–50', in Frank Crowley (editor), *A New History of Australia* (Melbourne: W Heinemann, 1974), 82. See further, H King, *Richard Bourke* (Melbourne, 1971).

5.   Roe, *ibid*, 87–88.

With this assumption—an exact reversal of the standard opinion of the ancient world—'the good' is always in 'the novel', since the novel, by definition, sheds the evils of a former age. Holding this belief strongly, political liberals have difficulty in according any intellectual credibility to views they deem 'conservative'. As recent examples, we could cite reactions to the 2004 return of 'conservative' Governments in both Australia and the USA, or the 2005 election of a 'conservative' Pope. In both cases, the political liberals tended to ask the question, 'what went wrong?' Since a move in a 'conservative' direction is a reversal of 'inevitable progress', it is, by definition (on this view), problematic.

Such political liberalism, of course, is alive and well in contemporary Australian society, and it also has its counterpart in church politics. However, from the point of view of the core Christian belief of repentance, it only takes a moment's reflection to realise its errors. From a Christian point of view, not all change is good, since not all change furthers God's cause in this world. This is especially true if, as the New Testament assumes, this world is opposed to its Creator. The belief in an inevitable progress towards a human utopia finds little biblical support. Instead, the gospel of Christ speaks of a God-driven movement towards the future kingdom of God. As a consequence, the gospel issues a call to all people everywhere to repent—not from all things *past*, but from all things *not good*.

2. Anglicanism and political repentance

2.1 Anglicanism and the local congregation

Anglican congregations exist throughout the world and are loosely associated primarily by virtue of their historical links to the Church of England. Congregations are associated geographically into Dioceses, and congregational representatives gather (usually annually) as Diocesan Synods. Dioceses are even more loosely associated into Provinces, and Diocesan representatives meet (even less regularly) as Provincial Synods. Relatively recently, three other meetings with international representation have gathered, with varying degrees of regularity (the Lambeth Conference, the Anglican Consultative Council, the Primate's Meeting). Because of the historical links with England, the Archbishop of Canterbury is also accorded a position of respect, but his role is clearly and explicitly different to that of the Pope in the Roman Catholic denomination. Some wish to tighten up such Anglican associations, and there is a tendency in some quarters to regard the pronouncements of the international or national bodies as more significant than those of local Synods, but the facts remain: Anglicanism is a loose association of loose associations—and perhaps even more so in Australia than in the rest of the world.[6]

The explicit 'theory' about Anglican churches states that 'the visible Church of Christ is *a congregation* of faithful men [ie persons], in which the pure Word of God is preached, and the Sacraments be duly ministered [. . .]' (*Articles of Religion*, XIX—my italics).[7] That is, the most important level is that of the local congregation. Anglican theory therefore enshrines the New Testament view of the church as the gathering of believers in a certain locality. Christ told his disciples that he is building his church (Matt 16:18), which looks towards the heavenly gathering of Christ's people around the throne of God and of the Lamb (cf Rev 4–5). The local gatherings of Christians are expressions of this heavenly reality, and they are instructed to see themselves from the heavenly point of view: they have been raised with Christ and their lives are hid with him at the right hand of God (Col 3:1–4; cf Eph 2). Whatever is done at the Diocesan, the Provincial, or even the International level of meetings, is certainly not 'church'. These denominational meetings find their legitimacy in supporting and promoting proper Christian relations and activities in the local congregations. When this is done appropriately, the denomination is worthwhile. When it is not, the denomination can become a persecutor of local congregations, and in so doing, outlives its usefulness.

On such an understanding, those 'below' (individual Christians and local congregations) have a responsibility to continue to act rightly, even when the denominational structures have acted wrongly. In this instance, there needs to be a call for repentance, issued 'from below' towards the institutions 'above'. But can an institutional decision be reversed? Can a denomination repent?

2.2 The theory of 'reception'

One of the features of the adoption of the ordination of women within some quarters of world-Anglicanism has been the formulation of the

---

6.   See BH Fletcher, 'Anglicanism in Sydney', http:/www.eppinganglicans.org.au/ outreach/fletcher_sydneyanglicanism_22may01.htm

7.   For further discussion of the church and Anglicanism, see the essays by DB Knox, in PG Bolt, MD Thompson, & R Tong (editors), *The Faith Once For All Delivered: An Australian Evangelical Response to The Windsor Report* (Camperdown, NSW: Australian Church Record, 2005), 81–86, 111–117.

notion of 'reception'. Although this arose in an earlier report associated with the Anglican Communion office,[8] 'reception' took on a particular prominence in the 2004 *Windsor Report,*[9] where it was regarded as an assumption of Anglican practice. 'Reception' is the label applied to the process by which an innovation instituted by one segment of the Anglican Communion can, over time, come to be accepted in other parts of the Anglican Communion. *The Windsor Report* was commissioned to respond to the consecration of a homo-sexual bishop in the Diocese of New Hampshire, USA, and the authorisation of the blessing of same sex unions by the Diocese of New Westminster, Canada. *The Windsor Report* took issue with the way in which these innovations occurred. The offending Dioceses should have followed the process put in place by the journey towards the ordination of women to the priesthood. Thus, the process of the 'reception' of the ordination of women has here become the assump-tion by which all other innovations are to be tested.[10]

There is no need here to critique or endorse this sanitised version of the situation within the Anglican Communion. However, given the position some now accord the notion of 'reception', it is worth noting that a legitimate consequence seems to be that it leaves room—at least in theory—for a political reversal.

If 'reception' is a process by which an innovation is discussed and examined at a political level, then, as a label, it is misleading. For, should the innovation prove unacceptable, it will not be received, but it will be rejected. To take this one step further, if the innovation has actually become operative in some quarters, and yet is found to be unacceptable, then this opens up the need for reversal of the practice.

---

8.   The 1985 Grindrod Report recommended it as an option, and the Lambeth Conference 1988 adopted the suggestion. The 'Eames Commission' was set up to monitor the 'reception' of the ordination of women to the priesthood, and to report to the 1998 Lambeth Conference. Archbishop Eames was also the chairman of the commission producing *The Windsor Report*.

9.   See www.anglicancommunion.org/windsor2004.

10. See *The Windsor Report*, pars 12–21, 68–69. For a brief critique of these paragraphs, and of the notion of 'reception', see P Bolt, M Thompson, & R Tong, 'The Windsor Report: An Outline with Commentary', and Jane Tooher, 'The Rhetoric of Reception: Lessons from the Ordination of Women Priests', in Bolt, Thompson & Tong, *op cit*, 13–15 and 67–69, respectively.

Even though this consequence has so far been largely ignored,[11] it seems that, in contrast to political liberalism's 'inevitability of progress', international Anglicanism now specifically allows for 'repentance'.

3. Repentance in the light of the coming kingdom

3.1 Repentance in the New Testament
The call for repentance has been a feature of the Christian movement from before it began. John the Baptist, in preparing Israel for the Coming One called upon Israel to repent in view of the coming kingdom of heaven (Matt 3:2), and called upon individual Israelites to 'bear fruit worthy of repentance' (Matt 3:8; Luke 3:8). In fact, the whole of his ministry was to prepare people 'with a view to repentance', before the Stronger One brought his 'baptism of spirit and fire' (Matt 3:11), and before the arrival of 'the forgiveness of sins' (Mark 1:4; Luke 3:3).

Jesus himself began his ministry by calling for repentance in the face of the coming Kingdom of God (Matt 4:17; Mark 1:15), explaining that he had come into the world to call sinners to repentance (Luke 5:32; Mark 2;17). He grieved over those who did not repent, in view of the danger this placed them under at the judgment day (Matt 11:20–21; 12:41; Luke 10:13; 11:32). On the other hand, as the Son of Man who came 'to seek and save the lost' (Luke 19:10), he revealed that the repentance of one sinner causes heaven to burst with joy (Luke 15:7, 10). Given the brevity of life, even tragic events can become object lessons that call upon the survivors to repent towards God, while time remains (Luke 13:3, 5; cf vv 7–10). In his famous parable of Dives and Lazarus, Jesus gives a sober warning that repentance will not come through signs and wonders, or even a resurrection, if God's word is not heeded (Luke 16:30–31). Since repentance towards God brings the forgiveness of sins, so, too, repentance towards one another should also be met with inter-personal forgiveness (Luke 17:3–4).

During his lifetime, Jesus had extended his ministry by sending out his disciples to call for repentance, just like he was doing (Mark 6:12). When he had risen from the dead, he then sent his chosen witnesses 'to preach in his name repentance with a view to the forgiveness of sins

---

11. It is discussed by Tooher, *op cit*, and seen in practice in *The Windsor Report*'s call for the innovators to express 'regret', and the subsequent call for a moratorium on their innovations.

into all nations beginning from Jerusalem' (Luke 24:47)— a mission which continues to our own day.

According to Acts, from the Day of Pentecost onwards, the apostles called for repentance (2:38) and for a turning from sins (3:19; 8:22). They spoke of the Risen Christ as the one 'God exalted to his right hand as Prince and Saviour in order to give to Israel repentance and the forgiveness of sins' (5:31). Before long, God's offer spilled over to the Gentiles (8:22), as the apostles realised after the conversion of Cornelius: 'then even to the Gentiles God has given repentance leading to life' (11:18). When the great apostle to the Gentiles himself began to preach, he recalled the ministry of John the Baptist who went before the Lord's arrival, calling for repentance from Israel (13:24; 19:4). When speaking before the Areopagus, Paul announced that, in the resurrection of Jesus Christ, God had demonstrated that the world would be judged through that man, and was now commanding 'all people everywhere to repent' (17:31). Paul summed up his own ministry in similar terms, saying that he had spent his time 'solemnly testifying to both Jews and Greeks about repentance towards God and faith in our Lord Jesus' (20:21), and that he had called upon both Jews and Gentiles 'to repent and to turn to God, doing works worthy of repentance' (26:20; cf Matt 3:8).

In his Epistle to the Romans, Paul cautions his readers about not taking advantage of the delay in the coming of God's judgment day, saying that this is part of the kindness of God affording opportunity for repentance (Rom 2:4)—a sentiment with which Peter also agreed (2 Peter 3:9).

Many in the ancient world, as in our own, confused repentance with remorse—the emotion of sorrow. Paul reminded the Corinthians of the difference: there is a sorrow that leads to repentance, but there is also a sorrow that does not; the former leads to life, but the latter leads only to death (2 Cor 7:9–10). As God's chosen apostle, Paul warns them that, upon his arrival, he will confront those who have not repented (2 Cor 12:21). Repentance is therefore important even for those who find themselves within Christian churches.

In the second letter to Timothy, the one who opposes the Lord's servant is said to be in the snare of the devil, and the Christian must instruct patiently and gently in the hope that 'God might give to them repentance that leads to the knowledge of the truth' (2 Tim 2:25).

The writer to the Hebrews sees 'repentance from dead works' as at the foundation of the Christian experience (Heb 6:1), and, in a saying particularly difficult to understand, he states that, for the one who falls away, it is impossible to renew them again to repentance (6:6), for their behaviour is tantamount to re-crucifying the Son of God with all the attendant shame. Esau apparently provides an OT illustration of this difficulty (Heb 12:17). The NT closes with a sustained call to repentance throughout John's Apocalypse (Rev 2:5, 16, 21–22; 3:3, 19; 9:20–21; 16:9, 11). In view of the imminent coming of Christ, bringing the eternal kingdom of God, repentance is rightly called for.

Repentance is a God-wrought change of mind, a change of the way in which the world is seen. Jesus once rebuked Peter for thinking like a human being, rather than like God (Mark 8:33). Repentance is to reverse this perspective on life. Seeing the world God's way introduces a profoundly *eschatological* perspective. That is, the future is dominated by the prospect of a judgment day, and the advent of God's eternal kingdom. Viewing the world in the perspective of these eternal realities, the repentant turn towards God's promised eternal joy, and so turn away from their sinful human thinking and behaviour.

3.2 A Theological account of repentance

Like most things, repentance has been variously understood—and misunderstood—throughout Church history. In reviewing this history, Robert Doyle has helpfully shown that there are basically two kinds of repentance.[12] 'Legal' repentance, viewing law as preceding grace, looks to things that have been done wrong and turns away from them in order to receive forgiveness for these breaches. On the other hand, evangelical repentance—that is, repentance that arises from the preaching of the gospel —is not so much a turning from sins in the first instance, but a turning to the God who has been gracious to us in Jesus Christ, which then entails leaving our sins behind. The gospel proclaims forgiveness to the sinner, on the basis of the work of Jesus Christ. Hearing of God's grace in Christ, the sinner is moved to put their trust in this gracious God. This movement towards God, entails a movement away from a godless life, and so a movement away from our sins. In retrospect, the Christian is now—from the standpoint of a

---

12.   Robert C Doyle, 'Repentance', in *Responding to the Gospel: Evangelical Perspectives on Christian Living*, edited by BG Webb (Explorations 9; Adelaide: Openbook, 1995), 15–39.

person 'in Christ'—ashamed of the former ways of life that only led to death (Rom 6:21). Perhaps we can say that, whereas legal repentance looks to a guilty past, evangelical repentance moves away from a guilty past, forgiven on the basis of Christ's work alone, being drawn towards God's glorious future.

3.3 Repentance in a larger framework

In other words, the gospel promises set repentance within a much larger framework than simply a transaction over things we have done wrong. Repentance is in the light of God's coming kingdom, and in response to the promise that God has granted all those in Christ a place in that new world.

The Kingdom of God will be the fulfilment of human longing for justice, and it will be the arrival of God's ancient promises of justice. God's justice is the 'setting right' of all things; the restoration of all things (Acts 3:21); the regeneration of all things (cf Matt 19:28); a 'new heaven and a new earth' (Rev 21–22). The arrival of the Son of God in our world, to live and die and rise again on our behalf, was the beginning of this future renewal. As the writer to the Hebrews put it, it was 'the time of reformation', a time of re-ordering of the world (Heb 9:10). When Titus is launched on his ministry in Crete, he is told—using a more intensified form of the same verb—to 'set in order' the things that remain (Titus 1:9). Although this has been narrowly understood of fixing up some local problems, it is best set against the broad sweep of New Testament eschatology, which then yields a profound view of Christian ministry. As the apostolic delegate (or those who later continue the apostolic ministry) engages in ministry amongst the local congregation, the world is being re-ordered according to the Creator's design.

This larger picture must also inform our understanding of the 'household tables' (eg Eph 5:21–6:4; Col 3:18–4:1; Titus 2; 1 Peter 2:17–3:9) and other passages which speak of properly-ordered relations between men and women. Rather than these relations being simply a reflection of ancient culture (which is so often asserted, rather than argued), these household relations were as radical in the ancient world as they are today. Here we see a snapshot of the Creator's design for properly ordered human life. The renovation of all things begins with Christian people, gathering together in Christian churches, being re-ordered according to the will of God.

In Jesus Christ, God launches his rescue plan for the world. Repentance results in God's re-ordering of life and relationships. God's good order restores us to our proper humanity.

Now, what has this to do with the ordination of women? Those who have stood for a male-only priesthood have done so in faithfulness to the biblical teaching. But this has not been in joyless, slavish obedience, as if the Scriptures are a new law to drive us to despair. This has been done in faithfulness to God's good word, in the belief that this is part of God's good order, and the belief that God's good order is best for his people, and best for the world. God's good order may be in stark contrast to contemporary culture, but the church of Christ has been called to 'think the things of God', and so to be counter-cultural, to demonstrate a different and better way of life, as men and women serve one another from the two sides of their complementary relations. This is God's good gift to us all.

4. The struggle for repentance

The reflection in this essay takes place within a situation committed to a male-only priesthood (with multiple ministries still available to women) as part of God's good order for his world. From this perspective, the 'struggle with respect to the ordination of women' is one that would seek the reversal of certain moves that have taken place at the level of denominational politics. Within Anglicanism, at least, the notion of 'reception' opens the door for such a reversal to take place. Repentance is possible at an institutional level.

But this reversal will only take place after there has been repentance at the more important level of the local churches and of individual believers. In the same way as for any other issue in life, we all need to re-examine the Scriptures and ask, what has God said about men, women, and ministry? If Sydney is any indication, these questions have not been talked about for a while.[13] Whereas these biblical and theological questions were discussed some twenty years

---

13. The 1992 Sydney Synod was informed by the Standing Committee that the 'substantial issues', that is, the biblical and theological arguments, had not been discussed by the Synod since 1985. The Scandrett v Dowling case switched the focus to legal-constitutional issues, see *1993 Year Book of the Diocese of Sydney*, 330–331. Arguably, this means there has been no discussion of 'substantial issues' for twenty years, and it is high time the next generation opened the questions again.

ago, they were then overtaken by legal and constitutional discussions. But the present generation needs to ask the question once again: what has God said, in his word, about men, women and ministry?

If political decisions have been made which are not appropriate in the light of his word, then repentance is called for, and repentance must be called for. For, in Jesus Christ God has begun to bring about a new world, and repentance begins the re-ordering of humanity, even before the kingdom arrives. With such joy set before us, why would we not want to step further into his marvellous light?

Reading Backward by Looking Forward: Baptists and the Ordination of Women

Stephen Spence
Adelaide

1. Introduction

The Baptist Church does not exist. This must be clearly understood in any discussion on Baptist practice, polity, and theology. Local Baptist churches exist. They may, and often do, choose to associate together for mutual support and to achieve things that they could not do as well on their own, for example theological education, community services, and cross-cultural mission. When local Baptist churches associate together, they form 'Unions' or 'Conventions'. In sociological terms, these Unions are rightly called denominations, with appointed leaders and associated infrastructure, but the ecclesiology of these churches does not change—they remain 'free churches'.[1] The South Australian Baptist Union (SABU) is one such union of churches; it is not *the* Baptist Church of South Australia. At no point does the local church lose its autonomy, its right to self-rule (under Christ).

Local Baptist churches discuss issues of theology and polity at Assembly, at which the various churches are represented and which acts as the governing body of the SABU. On the basis of these discussions, Assembly sets policies for the SABU and its ministries. Ordination to pastoral leadership is an area that the SABU member churches have agreed is an area of associational responsibility; that is, the SABU ordains at the direction of, and on behalf of, the local churches.[2] Local Baptist churches meeting in Assembly have agreed that gender is not an issue with respect to ordination, and this is the policy that governs the practice of SABU. However, local churches are

---

1. See below.
2. This is true for other Baptist Unions in Australia, but it is not the case for all Baptist Unions. Some Baptist churches ordain at the local level, and the association of Baptist churches to which they belong agree to mutually recognise these ordinations.

under no constitutional obligation to accept what the other local churches agree to in Assembly. Each local church is free to call to their positions of pastoral leadership whomever they believe God has chosen for them. Historical practice reveals that very rarely do local Baptist churches believe that God would choose for them a pastoral leader who is female. This explains why, while the South Australian Baptist Union agreed to ordain women to the ministry of pastoral leadership in 1974, there have only been three such ordinations, and in 2005 there is only one ordained female pastor employed by a local Baptist church in South Australia.

This freedom afforded to each local church means that it is not possible for anyone to say with precision 'what Baptists believe' about the ordination of women (or, any other issue debated generally among Evangelical Christians).[3] We have no creed, we have no confession, and we have no *magisterium*.

What follows in this article, therefore, is my understanding of what Baptists believe about the ordination of women.[4] I am a representative Baptist, but I am not a representative of Baptists. My opinions have been moulded by Baptist churches and by theological education in non-Baptist colleges. I am currently employed by the SABU as Principal of Burleigh College, a college begun in 1952 for the training of Baptist Men for the Ordained Ministry (note the capitals), which now educates Christian men and women for a wide variety of Christian service and leadership, including preparation for ordination to the ministry of pastoral leadership.

2. The Baptist theological ethos

Baptists are committed to a 'free church' ecclesiology.[5] Miroslav Volf argues that the free church is defined by the assertion, 'we—the people

---

3. A list of the fourteen major topics of debate within Evangelical Theology (with a brief discussion) can be found in R Olson, *The Westminster Handbook to Evangelical Theology* (Louisville: West-minster John Knox, 2004).

4. At times I will clearly stray into presenting what I think Baptists *should* believe. This, I am afraid, cannot be helped!

5. M Volf compares and contrasts the Free Church tradition with the Catholic and Orthodox in *After Our Likeness: The Church as the Image of the Trinity* (Grand Rapids: Eerdmans, 1998).

of God assembled in this particular place—are the church'. This assertion is not without its faults or limitations, but it does capture the Baptist vision of a local church as the body of Jesus Christ answerable to no one but its Lord. John Smyth (c 1565–1612), the first Baptist, expressed it this way, 'We say the Church or two or three faithful people Separated from the world and joyned together in a true covenant, have both Christ, the covenant, & promises, & the ministerial power of Christ given to them'.[6] Smyth puts the emphasis upon a covenanted community. Contemporary Baptists have tended to exchange this for a focus upon individual liberty of conscience. In this they have moved away from their theological heritage, but there is no understanding contemporary Baptists if one does not see how they have moved from a free church to a free conscience. This tends to mean that Baptist churches are slow to change. It is neither the mind of its leaders nor the bylaws of its organising documents that need to be changed but the minds of its many members. Charles W Dewesse writes for an American *Baptist History and Heritage Society,*

> Put simply, every individual is responsible only to God in matters of conscience—not to the state, not to the church, not to creedal statements, not to pastors, not to seminary presidents, not to denominational leaders, not even to one another. True faith is voluntary.[7]

Baptists share many beliefs and practices despite the plurality of voices among Christians who attend Baptist churches and the historical variety among Baptist churches in issues of polity such as baptism and membership. Anyone who has had occasion to worship with or dialogue with Baptists from around Australia or from around the world will surely have noticed this.[8] Baptists can generally be expected to be Evangelicals. Evangelicalism is, of course, a much-disputed term. In Baptist circles it tends to indicate someone who is committed to conversionism: 'the belief that lives need to be changed'; activism: 'the expression of the gospel in effort'; biblicism: the Scriptures are seen as 'the supreme authority for faith, the primary

---

6.   Cited in Volf, *After Our Likeness*, 10.

7.   http://www.baptisthistory.org/pamphlets/freedom.htm, 21 March 2005.

8.   The Baptist World Alliance, of which the Baptist Union of Australia is a member, includes national unions and conventions from 120 countries.

source for shaping their theology and nurturing their spiritual growth'; and crucicentrism: an 'emphasis on the doctrine of the cross as the focus of the gospel and the fulcrum of a theological system'.[9] This commitment to Scripture as the 'supreme authority' and 'primary source', together with our emphasis upon personal liberty in interpreting Scripture, means that individual Baptist churches believe in their own competence to read the Scriptures in order to determine God's plan for their church.

The SABU would never attempt to subvert the local church's attempt to discover God's will for it through a careful study of Scripture. Indeed, the SABU constitution states, as the basis of the voluntary association of local Baptist churches,

> That our Lord and Saviour, Jesus Christ, God manifest in the flesh, is the sole and absolute authority in all matters of faith and practice. These are revealed in and through the Scriptures, both Old and New Testaments. Each church has the liberty and responsibility, through the revelation of the Holy Spirit, to interpret, to preach, and to administer Christ's will in these matters.

This is an excellent attempt to balance the role of the word, the Spirit, and the community in identifying the Lord's authority over his people. However, in stressing the liberty and responsibility of each local church to interpret and administer Christ's will, it fails to require local churches to take note of what God is saying to and through the other local churches.[10] There can be no attempt by the churches meeting in Assembly to coerce or direct local churches with respect to their faith or practice. Only when an individual church persists in some

---

9. DW Bebbington, *Evangelicalism in Modern Britain: A History from the 1730s to the 1980s* (London: Unwin Hyman, 1989). According to Mark A Knoll, this is 'one of the most useful general definitions of the [evangelical] phenomenon'; *The Scandal of the Evangelical Mind* (Grand Rapids: Eerdmans, 1994), 8.

10. This 'failure' can be considered a falling from the fullness of free church ecclesiology (as described by M Volf). However, to most Baptists, it is an essential means of maintaining the autonomy of the local church.

gross violation of what the other churches are willing to concede as acceptable Baptist faith and practice might action be taken to expel a church from the SABU family.[11]

3. Reading Scripture as Baptists

With no official body or manual capable of determining Baptist polity, Baptists have embraced the metaphor of the Bible as the instruction manual for the church. The largest Baptist association of churches in the world, the Southern Baptist Convention (SBC), states in Article One of The Baptist Faith and Message Statement (2000), 'The Holy Bible . . . is a perfect treasure of divine instruction; . . . the supreme standard by which all human conduct, creeds, and religious opinions should be tried.'

This approach to establishing polity by attempting to get back to the Bible has been characteristic of Baptist churches since their formation. While all the churches of the Reformation attempted to break from what they saw as the corrupt practices of the Catholic Church, the Baptists were among those who most sought to start afresh. Not to start again (as if from scratch), but to start afresh—to recover the church of the New Testament and to model itself upon it. (John Smyth believed that, because there were no contemporary churches that were faithful to the gospel, he needed to baptise himself.[12]) For the early Baptists and for their heirs, the goal of Baptist church polity was to reproduce as faithfully as possible the church of the New Testament. In the 1970s, in the Baptist church in which I grew up, this was seen as both desirable and possible.

Article Six of the SBC's 'Baptist Faith and Message Statement' states, 'While both men and women are gifted for service in the church, the office of pastor is limited to men as qualified by Scripture.' It seems to me that those who framed 'as qualified by Scripture' in Article Six assumed that the house-churches of the NT world and the leadership structures of those house-churches would be somehow like the way SBC churches do church now. Yet here lies the problem with the 'Bible as instruction manual' hermeneutic. Neither the church nor the 'office of pastor' in NT times can be identified with contemporary SBC

---

11.   'Gross violation' is not easily defined, but we expect that we will know it when we see it!

12.   He later came to regret this and submitted himself to baptism by a Mennonite preacher.

churches.[13] In order to read the instruction manual, some form of cultural translation is required.

An obvious example of such a cultural translation is the identification of 'I permit no woman to teach or to have authority over a man; she is to keep silent' in 1 Timothy 2:12 with 'I do not permit any woman to hold the pastoral office in a local church'. The problem is two-fold. One, Paul could not have had in mind the pastoral office as we practice it today. And two, it would be a rare Baptist indeed who would allow that simply because a person is ordained that person has 'authority' over them and they must accept their 'teaching'. 'Authority lies with the Scriptures not with some would-be Baptist Pope!'[14] Paul's instructions to Timothy and his church do not, *without interpretation*, apply to the ordination debate. The problem is that the instructional manual does not have a section on 'women in ordained ministry'. It does not even have a section on 'ordained ministry'.[15] This metaphor of the instruction manual is inadequate and needs to be abandoned. It tempts us to read our issues into the NT text rather than to discover the issues that the text is attempting to address.[16]

A phenomenological reading of the New Testament would suggest that its genre is closer to 'historical narrative' than 'instruction manual'; its instructions are always applied first to a concrete historical situation. In a modernist world in which truth was (and is for many contemporary Baptists) understood as best expressed through propositions, Baptist churches often read church polity from Scripture without reference to its narrative context. The goal of a modernist

---

13. Robert Banks provides a narrative account of a first-century church in *Going to Church in the First Century* (second edition; Paramatta: Hexagon, 1985).

14. In this context 'Pope' is being used pejoratively rather than as an attempt to fairly represent the understanding and practice of the Roman Catholic Church.

15. This has caused some Baptists to reject ordination itself, eg in the Western Australian Baptist Union; but even when this has been done it has not led to a subsequent increase in the number of women in leadership.

16. As an exegetical principle, only once the issues of the text in its historical context have been understood are we able to apply the text to our contemporary situation, thus ensuring we have correctly translated what it is saying.

instruction manual hermeneutic is to find a proposition and generalise it. (However, this is not done without reference to current practice. There is no member SABU church that requires women to keep silent on the basis of 1 Timothy 2:12. Why?) Thus the attempt is made to make one of the propositions contained within 1 Timothy 2:12 into the interpretive key that will unlock the answer to our question of 'women and ordained ministry'. This, I would argue, is because we have made the text answer a question it is not asking. We have failed to find the question it is addressing and thus we have failed to be formed by its word.[17]

4. The practice of one New Testament church

The first-century church that I know best is the church in Rome.[18] This church was founded some ten years or so after Pentecost, initially within the synagogues of Rome, when Jewish Christians followed the trade routes from the east and brought their new faith in Jesus with them. By the time Paul wrote to the church in Rome in 57 CE, there might have been between 250 and 500 Christians[19] meeting in a network of house-churches dominated by Gentile converts (and thus separated from on-going involvement in the synagogues). These Gentile converts had chosen to belong to Christian house-churches rather than accepting Jewish proselytism and joining the synagogue. Their practices and their sympathies lay not with Jewish practices but with the cultural values they knew best. In his letter to them, Paul rebukes the Gentile majority for their arrogance towards the Jews and challenges them to be sensitive to the 'weaknesses' of their brother and sisters. He calls all Christians, Gentiles and Jews, to 'the obedience of faith' (1:5), to a life lived through walking with the Spirit (8:4).

---

17. I would suggest that 1 Timothy is addressing the issue of how our actions—eg the actions of quarrelling men, domineering women, conceited leaders, self-indulgent widows, slaves, and those who desire wealth—can bring the gospel into disrepute and so hinder the church's witness to the God 'who desires everyone to be saved and to come to the knowledge of the truth' (2:4). Now that will preach!

18. I am not arguing that the church in Rome is either the most important church of the first-century or even that it is representative of all other first-century churches. Rather, given Paul's approval of it (Rom 1:8–12), its practices represent a valid expression of acceptable church polity.

19. The population of Rome is estimated to have been about one million. The Jewish community may have numbered between 30,000 and 40,000.

Little is said about the practice or the structure of their worshiping communities. However, certain values can be discerned from Paul's list of greetings contained in chapter 16.[20] It is likely that Paul knew at least twelve of the twenty-six people greeted in his letter.[21] He evidently knew the importance of those he did not know personally, for the decision to name these people in his first letter to the Christians in Rome suggests that these are people of significance within the Christian community. In particular, some are noted for their work for the Lord (*synergos* in 16:3, 9 and *kopian* in 16:6, 12 [bis]). Among these prominent Roman Christian workers are five women: Prisca, Mary, Tryphaena and Tryphosa, and Persis. (By comparison, only three men are named in this group: Aquila, Andronicus, and Urbanus.[22])

While Paul identifies these people by their work in the Lord rather than by titles, the significance of their leadership role within the community should not be diminished. Paul uses the same terms to identify Timothy (*synergos* in 16:21) and his own labours for Christ (*kopian* in, for example, Phil 2:16, 1 Cor 15:10). Mary's work is specifically identified as 'among you' (16:6), that is, among 'all God's beloved in Rome, called to be saints' (1:7). There is no apparent distinction between the work done by the wife and husband in the team composed of Prisca and Aquila (16:3) although, based upon the culturally unusual practice of naming the wife first, Lampe concludes, 'Apparently, Prisca was more prominent in community activity than her husband.'[23]

The appearance in Paul's list of greetings of Andronicus and Junia, whom Paul identifies as both 'my relatives who were in prison with me . . . [who] were in Christ before I was' and 'who are prominent among the apostles' (16:7), suggests that females in prominent leadership roles within the Christian community was not unique to Rome. (There is no possibility that 'apostle' could be used for a purely local office.) This greeting is so significant for any discussion of the

---

20. The evidence that chapter 16 was part of the original letter addressed to the Romans is overwhelming; see P Lampe, *From Paul to Valentinus: Christians at Rome in the First Two Centuries,* translated by M Steinhauser; Minneapolis: Fortress, 2003), 153–64.
21. *Ibid,* 167–8.
22. Lampe includes Rufus' mother and two males, Apelles and Rufus, as possible additions to this list (*ibid,* 165–6).
23. *Ibid,* 167.

leadership role of women in the early church that Junia has had both her gender and her position among the apostles unfairly questioned.

With respect to her gender, Lampe notes, 'The church fathers of late antiquity correctly perceived that Andronicus's companion was not a man. This changed only with Aegidius of Rome (1245-1316 CE).'[24]

> The case for reading the female name Junia rather than the male name Junias in Romans 16:7 has been made adequately in scholarship since the 1970s and has been widely accepted, while the REB and NRSV are, I believe, the first English translations to place 'Junia' in the text and relegate 'Junias' to a footnote.[25]

Even the conservative scholar TR Schreiner writes that 'the likely conclusion is that Junia is a woman, though certainty is impossible'.[26]

Many have interpreted the phrase 'who are prominent among the apostles' (16:7) as meaning that Junia (and Andronicus) were well known to, or well regarded by, the apostles. That is, Junia was a female but not an apostle. However, the scholarly consensus is again strongly in favour of reading these words as indicating that Paul considers this couple as apostles. CEB Cranfield comments that it is virtually certain that the phrase 'outstanding among the apostles' means 'outstanding in the group who may be designated apostles'.[27] A recent detailed case, taking into account the latest views to the contrary, can be found in Richard Bauckham, *Gospel Women* (2003).[28] Schreiner also concludes that while Junia and Andronicus are not placed by Paul among 'the

---

24. *Ibid*, 166 n 39. In fact, Lampe argues that those who reject Junia in favour of a masculine Junias have accepted 'an embarrassing solution fabricated by men'. See also RR Schulz, "Romans 16:7: Junia or Junias?," *ExpTim* 98 (1986–1987): 108–10.

25. RJ Bauckham, *Gospel Women: Studies in the Named Women of the Gospels* (Grand Rapids: Eerdmans, 2002), 166.

26. *Romans* (ECNT; Grand Rapids: Baker Books, 1998), 796.

27. *A Critical and Exegetical Commentary on the Epistle to the Romans* (sixth edition; ICC; Edinburgh: T&T Clark, 1975–1979), 789.

28. Bauckham, *Gospel Women*, 172-80. The detail provided by Bauckham is in response to the arguments of MH Burer and DB Wallace, 'Was Junia Really an Apostle? A Re-examination of Rom 16.7', *NTS* 47.1 (2001): 76–91, who attempt to change the recent scholarly consensus.

ranks of the Twelve', nor did they 'exercise the same kind of authority as Paul, Barnabas, or James', they are rightly called apostles.[29]

Yet Schreiner goes on to assert, 'As a female missionary Junia may have directed her energies especially to other women.' But as any reader of commentaries will know, the word 'may' at this point indicates that Schreiner has gone beyond the text.[30] He justifies his speculation on the basis of Käsemann's remark, 'The wife can have access to the women's areas, which would not be generally available to the husband' and on 'the Pauline admonition in 1 Tim 2:12'.[31] Neither of these is a sufficient basis upon which to curtail the scope of Junia's apostleship.

As an apostle, Paul did not feel the need to take a female companion with him in order for him to preach and teach the gospel to women. Why would Andronicus need a wife for this purpose? In fact, as has been adequately demonstrated, by meeting in the homes of Christians the early church was meeting in 'female space' (in contrast to the 'male space' of the public sphere).[32] It was in the home that women could exercise positions of leadership.

> The most direct points of contact with the role of the *pater familias* are the Pauline house-church patrons, both men and women . . . Especially noteworthy is the appearance of a number of women house-church patrons within Paul's Aegean mission sphere. They must be women of independent means who manage their own households as *mater familias*.[33]

L Michael White notes that the terms associated with work and labour are regularly used by Paul to honour the efforts of his patrons,

---

29. *Ibid*, 796–97.
30. Schreiner, *Romans*, 797.
31. *Ibid*.
32. KJ Torjesen, *When Women Were Priests: Women's Leadership in the Early Church and the Scandal of Their Subordination in the Rise of Christianity* (San Francisco: Harper, 1993), especially 53–87.
33. LM White, 'Paul and Pater Familias', *Paul in the Greco-Roman World: A Handbook*, edited by JP Sampley (Harrisburg: Trinity, 2003), 467.

the house-church leaders. These terms are used in Romans 16 of both men and women.[34]

Schreiner's appeal to 1 Timothy overlooks the more proximate, and therefore more relevant, textual examples of Prisca,[35] Mary, Tryphaena, Tryphosa, and Persis (and Phoebe[36]). Schreiner is attempting to create theological conformity in the midst of historical diversity. He alludes to Moo who accepts,

> Ministry in the early church was never confined to men; these greetings and other similar passages show that women engaged in ministries that were just as important as those of men. We have created many problems for ourselves by confining 'ministry' to what certain full-time Christian workers do. But it is important that we do not overinterpret this evidence either. For nothing Paul says in this passage (even in v.7) conflicts with limitations on some kinds of women's ministry with respect to men such as I think are suggested by 1 Tim 2:8–15 and other texts.[37]

But Moo has *under*interpreted the evidence of Romans 16. On what textual basis does he believe that women 'engaged in ministries *that were just as important as those of men*'? The text does not speak of two (or more) types of ministries of equal importance but of coworkers and labourers—those who participate in the same ministry as Paul—who

---

34.   *Ibid.*

35.   We know Prisca was one of the people responsible for the teaching of Apollos (Acts 18:26).

36.   Phoebe is commended to the Romans by Paul as a 'deacon of the church at Cenchreae [near Corinth] . . . for she has been a benefactor of many and of myself as well' (Rom 16:1–2; NRSV). Phoebe was evidently a significant leader of the Corinthian church who was privileged to carry Paul's letter to Rome and act as his representative of some sort. See the discussion in B Witherington III, *Paul's Letter to the Romans: A Socio-Rhetorical Commentary* (Grand Rapids: Eerdmans, 2004), 382–85). That such a person could act for Paul suggests that the Roman church accepted females in positions of responsibility within the Christian community.

37.   D Moo, *The Epistle to the Romans* (NICNT; Grand Rapids: Eerdmans, 1996), 927.

happen to be both female and male. On the basis of Romans 16 it is impossible to distinguish between what Mary (and Tryphaena, Tryphosa, and Persis) did in labouring (*kopiao*) for the Lord and what Paul did for the Lord. It is impossible to distinguish what Prisca did from what Aquila or Urbanus did as co-labourers (*synergoi*) with Paul. It is impossible to distinguish what Junia did from what Andronicus did to win prominence among the apostles. There is no 'women's ministry' in Romans any more than there is 'men's ministry'. There is only 'labour' for the Lord. But this comes as no surprise to readers of Romans, for Paul has already written in 12:3–8 that all Christians are recipients of 'gifts that differ according to the grace given to us' (v 6)—as Schreiner rightly notes, 'no member of the church is exempt, for every believer has been given a measure of faith and is called on to estimate himself or herself in accord with the apportioned faith'. These gifts are to be exercised for the benefit of the whole body of Christ. The limitations addressed in 1Timothy 2:12 are more correctly described as being placed upon some women than upon 'some kinds of women's ministry'. (Exploring who those women are and why they are being limited in their ministry would take us beyond the church in Rome.)

Romans 16 does not tell us about the organisational structure of the house-churches of Rome. It certainly doesn't address the issue of 'ordination to *the* Baptist ministry'. But it does show that women laboured alongside Paul and other Christian men in the common cause of the gospel. It even suggests that, in Rome, it was the women who were the more prominent among the workers in the early Christian community.

Paul's letter to the Romans gives us ample historical evidence to accept women into positions of leadership within the church in the same roles as men. But this doesn't actually answer the question, What should our church do? How do we move from knowing what is permissible to implementing what is desirable for God's church?

5. Back to the Bible by looking to the *eschaton*

The debates in Baptist churches about women in leadership are, superficially, biblical arguments. However, too much biblical scholarship has demonstrated the reality of women leaders in the early church for anyone to believe that historical exegesis is not being supplanted by theological or cultural values. We read from within the distinct culture of our own faith community, looking for validation of our accepted practices. (Or, in some contexts, looking for ammunition to negate our community's accepted practices.) This does not mean that the hermeneutical task of reading Scripture is hopelessly circular. Rather, it points us to the need for a hermeneutical spiral: an on-going reading of the text that continues to challenge the pre-judgments that we brought to the previous reading of the text.

But—and here I might part from many of my fellow Baptists—in which direction should the hermeneutical spiral spin? Back towards the first-century past or forward to the *eschaton*? My understanding of the diversity of the first-century church convinces me that the New Testament does not prescribe church practice and polity; it rather describes an historical diversity. With this assumption, there is no point attempting to spiral back towards an imaginary 'golden past'. Rather, we should be spiralling forward to the hope-filled escha-tological future. This is what I see happening in the churches of the first-century. They sought to live in the light of the eschatological glory of the established kingdom, a light in which 'there is no longer Jew or Greek, there is no longer slave or free, there is no longer male and female; for all of you are one in Christ Jesus' (Gal 3:28). They didn't always get there, for they were as limited by their culture and their sin as we are; but they knew the direction they were to travel. They didn't claim to have discovered a timeless and acultural pattern of being church (certainly, no such claim has been preserved in the New Testament canon), but they did speak hopefully of what was to come. And they did hold that future up against their practices in order to judge whether they were being true to their calling.

Paul's letter to the Romans demonstrates this perspective of eschatological glory to judge present practices. Paul challenges the Christians of Rome to unity, to bearing with the failings of the weak, and to mutual edification—all areas of present failure for the church in Rome—by an appeal to Scripture. 'For whatever was written in former days was written for our instruction, so that by steadfastness and by the encouragement of the scriptures we might have hope' (15:4). This appeal to Scripture looks forward, not back:

> 'Therefore I will confess you among the Gentiles, and
> sing praises to your name'; and again he says, 'Rejoice,
> O Gentiles, with his people'; and again, 'Praise the
> Lord, all you Gentiles, and let all the peoples praise
> him'; and again Isaiah says, 'The root of Jesse shall

come, the one who rises to rule the Gentiles; in him the
Gentiles shall hope. (Rom 15:9–12)

This was never the historical experience of the people of God. It
was always the deep hope of God's people. For Paul, the eschaton had
begun to break into the midst of God's people through the resurrection
of Jesus and the subsequent bestowal of the Spirit. His challenge to the
church of Rome was to live in the light of their future hope.

The 'people of the Book', as we like to think of ourselves, are still
people of hope. Our hope is for a time when all people will stand as
one in Christ Jesus, without reference to their ethnicity, their social
status, or their gender. We need to learn to read the Scriptures with our
eyes opened by the future, not closed by the past, so that we 'abound
in hope' (Rom 15:13).

Recognising the Ministry of Women

Philip Wilson
Adelaide

For over a century now feminist advocates and scholars have been persuading humanity to recognise the equal dignity of women and to reshape social structures in the light of this recognition. From the perspective of the leadership of the Roman Catholic Church, Pope John XXIII first acknowledged the significance of this movement, speaking of it as a distinctive characteristic of his day that could bring people to 'a better knowledge of the true God'.[1] Today Catholic teaching unambiguously regards both women and men as created in God's image: both 'are equally capable of receiving the outpouring of divine truth and love in the Holy Spirit'.[2] Discussion about the equal dignity of women in the church often turns to the issue of the ordination of women. I want to propose in this paper that an important letter from Pope John Paul II in another field can help to advance reflection on this issue and to grapple with some of the difficulties it raises.

John Paul II's encyclical letter *Ut Unum Sint* has provided a rich source of reflection for the churches and the ecumenical movement.[3] It urges all Christians and especially Catholics, while holding to the deepest truths of faith, to overcome past misunderstandings and misgivings and work for the unity that Christ wants for the church. Most strikingly, the pope has called church leaders and theologians to dialogue about the exercise of the papal ministry. The momentous nature of this call is reflected in the strong response of two scholars known for their careful use of language. Cardinal Walter Kasper, President of the Pontifical Council for Promoting Christian Unity, sees this invitation as 'a revolutionary step for a pope', and theologian Hermann Pottmeyer believes that it has 'inaugurated a new era in the

---

1. Pope John XXIII, *Pacem in Terris* (Boston, Mass: St Paul Books & Media, 1963), n 41, 45.
2. Pope John Paul II, *Mulieris Dignitatem* (Homebush, NSW: St Paul Publications, 1988), n 16.
3. Pope John Paul II, *Ut Unum Sint* (Homebush, NSW: St Pauls, 1995).

history of Christianity'.[4] Both look forward to an ecumenical Petrine ministry—a hope that has already found confirmation from the Anglican—Roman Catholic International Commission. In *The Gift of Authority*, the commission states: 'such a primacy could be offered and received even before our churches are in full communion . . . We envisage a primacy that will even now help to uphold the legitimate diversity of traditions, strengthening and safeguarding them in fidelity to the Gospel'.[5]

The pope's invitation to dialogue about the Petrine ministry has three integral elements. First, it recognises that at times in history the exercise of the papal ministry has contributed to events which have caused other Christians difficulty with this ministry of unity.[6] He adds a little later: 'for a great variety of reasons, and against the will of all concerned, what should have been a service sometimes manifested itself in a very different light'.[7] John Paul II joins Paul VI in asking forgiveness for these events. Second, in calling for dialogue about the exercise of an ecumenical Petrine ministry, the pope is 'in no way renouncing what is essential to its mission' according to Catholic teaching.[8] Rather, he wants to faithfully preserve this ministry. And thirdly, he hopes that the dialogue he invites will lead to a new situation, which he sees prefigured in the communion of faith and sacramental life of the first millennium, in which the Bishop of Rome had a crucial ministry of unity.

How, then, can we hold on to what is essential in the Catholic understanding of the Petrine ministry while moving toward the new situation envisioned by the John Paul II? Kasper argues that in order to advance the visible unity of the church, four principles should govern

---

4. Walter Kasper, 'A Discussion on the Petrine Ministry', *That They May All Be One: The Call to Unity Today* (London: Burns & Oates, 2004), 138; Hermann J Pottmeyer, *Toward a Papacy in Communion: Perspectives from Vatican Councils I & II*, translated by Matthew J O'Connell (New York: Herder & Herder, 1998), 13.

5. Anglican Catholic International Commission, *The Gift of Authority: Authority in the Church III* (London: Catholic Truth Society, 1999), n 60.

6. Pope John Paul II, *Ut Unum Sint*, n 88.

7. Pope John Paul II, *Ut Unum Sint,* n 95.

8. Pope John Paul II, *Ut Unum Sint*, n 95.

the interpretation of Catholic dogmas about primacy.[9] Firstly, they should be interpreted within the context of a rich theology of church, particularly in relationship to understandings of Christ and the Trinity. Secondly, these dogmas should be interpreted in the light of the whole tradition of faith of the church through the centuries. Here he believes that the theology of *communio* that dominated the ecclesiology of the first millennium and was retrieved by Vatican II will be particularly fruitful. Thirdly, the Petrine ministry must be interpreted according to the gospel. After discussing the relationship between biblical exegesis and church tradition Kasper concludes that the Petrine ministry cannot be understood as power, 'but only as service'.[10] And fourthly, interpretations of Catholic dogmas about primacy must take into account 'the historical context of a dogma and the historical meaning of the concepts used by it'.[11] The historical form of a dogma can contain elements that obscure its essential content in a new age.

My contention is that John Paul II's call to rethink the exercise of papal primacy and Kasper's principles of interpretation offer a way of approaching the issue of the ordination of women. The pope's distinction—between what is essential, needing to be faithfully preserved, and what must be renewed in the light of this new context—is also important for the life of the church when considering the meaning of ordination. I want to hold faithfully to the essential teaching of the magisterium on this issue while finding a way forward on the question of women's ministry and also on the way in which we understand ordination in the church. Streamlining Kasper's principles, I am proposing that priestly ordination be approached from a dual perspective. Any faithful understanding of its meaning for today must interpret it in a coherent and integrated fashion: according to the gospel, taking into account the whole tradition of faith, and in relationship to the hierarchy of truths of faith. And secondly, a faithful understanding of the meaning of ordination must recognise the limitations of its previous expressions and not only let go of but also actively work to right those practices and understandings which obscure the doctrine's fuller meaning. To address this question, I will initially turn to the

---

9.   Kasper, 'A Discussion of the Petrine Ministry', 141–9. I have slightly altered the order of Kasper's principles.

10. Kasper, 'A Discussion on the Petrine Ministry', 147.

11. Kasper, 'A Discussion of the Petrine Ministry', 145.

second of these: the limitations of previous expressions of priestly ministry. In the following section I will pick up the first perspective by briefly presenting an important theology of the church at Vatican II—that of *communio*.

1. Addressing cultural limitations

I have already pointed out that it is only over the last century that western culture, in particular, has been engaged in the process of recognising the equal dignity of women. For the greatest part of western Christian history the paradigm of patriarchy has not only shaped political, social and family structures—men ruling over women; women and children being the property of husbands and fathers—it has also shaped Christian practice and theology, even understandings of God.[12] In the last three hundred years a new understanding of the human person in society has evolved, built on the values of liberty and equality. The American and French revolutions are pivotal events in the establishment of the modern worldview. From the end of the eighteenth century this worldview has undergone a double expansion. It has spread from western Europe and America to an increasing number of states, and it has expanded in intensity, affecting increasingly more aspects of life in these states, including not only gender but also class, race, age and disability among others.

Biblical scholars and theologians have made it clear that the modern recognition of the equal dignity of women rather than contradicting Christian faith finds strong resonance in the practice of Jesus' ministry, the range of biblical images for God, and the life of the early church. Many aspects of Jesus' life and ministry reflect a stance opposed to the patriarchal culture in which he lived: his openness to women and their inclusion as disciples, his friendship with Mary and Martha and Mary Magdalene, the presence of women at the cross, and the role of women as the first witnesses of the resurrection.[13] Through his parables, healings and meals Jesus ushers in the kingdom of God,

---

12. Anne Carr outlines these matters in *Transforming Grace: Christian Tradition and Women's Experience* (San Francisco: Harper & Row, 1988), 135-8.

13. See, for example, Anne Carr, *Transforming Grace*, chapter 8; Elizabeth A Johnson, *Consider Jesus: Waves of Renewal in Christology* (New York: Crossroad, 1996), chapters 4 and 7.

into which all people are invited, especially those regarded in his time as outcasts.[14] In his encyclical on the dignity and vocation of women, John Paul II traces the role of women in the gospel emphasising: 'In all of Jesus' teaching, as well as in his behaviour, one can find nothing which reflects the discrimination against women prevalent in his day. On the contrary, *his words and works always express the respect and honour due to women'.*[15]

Many New Testament scholars believe that Galatians 3.26–28 reflects the egalitarian ethos of the early Christian community both before Paul and as preached by Paul:

> For in Jesus Christ you are all children of God through faith. As many of you as were baptised into Christ have clothed yourselves with Christ. There is no longer Jew or Greek, there is no longer slave or free, there is no longer male and female; for all of you are one in Christ Jesus.

In her study of this passage Elisabeth Schüssler Fiorenza concludes that it extols 'the oneness of the body of Christ, the church, where all social, cultural, religious, national, and biological gender divisions and differences are overcome and all structures of domination are rejected'.[16] Toward the final section of *Mulieris Dignitatem*, John Paul II exegetes a passage from Ephesians 5 including the lines: 'Be subject to one another out of reverence to Christ. Wives, be subject to your husbands as you are to the Lord' (vv 21,22). Although this whole passage is permeated with the language of subjection, which the pope says belongs to the first-century worldview, he insists that the emphasis of the text is on mutuality. He maintains that the text expresses the equality of husband and wife understood in the early Christian community—equality brought about by what he calls 'the innovation

---

14. This theme is developed in Edward Schillebeeckx, *Jesus: An Experiment in Christology*, translated by Hubert Hoskins (New York: Crossroad, 1979), 179–270.

15. Pope John Paul II, *Mulieris Dignitatem*, n 13–16, at 14 (emphasis in original).

16. Elisabeth Schüssler Fiorenza, *In Memory of Her: A Feminist Theological Reconstruction of Christian Origins* (London: SCM Press, 1983), 208–18 at 218.

of the Gospel'. Commenting on the passage, he says: 'The "innovation" of Christ is a fact: it constitutes the unambiguous content of the evangelical message and is the result of the Redemption'.[17] He believes that the Ephesians text reflects the same practice of equality in the early Christian community that is found in the Galatians text discussed above.

In summary, any consideration of the question of whether it is possible for the Roman Catholic Church to ordain women takes place in a fundamentally different context in the twenty-first century than it may have had in the nineteenth or before. The movement to recognise the equal dignity of women has not only advanced our understanding of the human person and society, it has also led to a clearer understanding of the gospel message and the life of discipleship to which the gospel summons us. In the discourse about equal dignity two essential principles are held together: those of equality and difference. Firstly, in this movement there is a 'universalist' call to acknowledge that all people possess equal rights and entitlements, and that what must be opposed at all costs is the existence of first and second-class human beings. Secondly, the movement to recognise women's equal dignity is not an effort to ensure that the pattern of men's lives is replicated in women's. Rather, the movement calls for recognition of women's unique identity. The movement is born out of the experience that this distinctiveness has been ignored, glossed over and assimilated into the patriarchal culture of the day.[18] I believe that any response to the question of the ordination of women in the Roman Catholic tradition must recognise the equal and unique dignity of women.

A further historical factor that must be taken into account when considering the question of the ordination of women is the prevailing theology and practice of the priesthood on the eve of the Second Vatican Council. Prior to the Council, one particular view of priesthood dominated the church's understanding of ministry for almost a millennium: a view commonly referred to as the monarchical

---

17. Pope John Paul II, *Mulieris Dignitatem*, 24.
18. Edward Collins Vacek surveys feminist scholarship and Vatican teaching on the language of equality, difference and complementarity in 'Feminism and the Vatican', *Theological Studies* 66 (March 2005): 159–77.

or pyramidal model.[19] It was the result of a long and complex history
that included a development in the project of Christendom during the
eleventh century, the Roman Catholic Church's response to the
Reformation in the sixteenth century and its response to the
Enlightenment in the nineteenth century. The view of ministry that
emerged through these phases saw all the specific ministerial gifts of
the Spirit concentrated in the priest. Edward Schillebeeckx points out
that as a consequence, believers 'ceased to be the subjects of faith, in
the Spirit, and were reduced to being the object of priestly care'.[20]
Being passive receptors, 'laity', as they became known at the beginning
of this process, did not see themselves as sharing in the ministerial gifts
of the Spirit. And further, what the New Testament understood in
terms of ministerial service found expression primarily in terms of
power and jurisdiction from the medieval period onward. Lost from
view in the pre-conciliar understanding of priesthood, therefore, was
not only its essential connection with the gospel call to service, but also
the integral relationship between ordained ministry and the ministry
of all the baptised.

This is not to idealise the first millennium and to denigrate the
second. Christian faith profoundly transformed western culture in the
second millennium, even though at times in this period the fusion of
faith and culture had effects that were the antithesis of the gospel. It is,
however, to recognise that a rich understanding of the relationship
between ordained ministry and the ministry of the baptised present in
the first millennium was lost in the second. I believe that the theology
of *communio* retrieved by the Second Vatican Council (the same
theology that Cardinal Kasper believes is central to a renewed
understanding of the Petrine ministry), will be crucial to a renewed
understanding of the priesthood in the twenty-first century. It is to that
that I now turn.

---

19.   Among other works in this area, see: Edward Schillebeeckx, *The Church
      with a Human Face: A New and Expanded Theology of Ministry*,
      translated by John Bowden (London: SCM Press, 1985), 203-8;
      Schillebeeckx, *Church: The Human Story of God*, translated by John
      Bowden (London: SCM Press, 1990), 198-207; Susan K Wood,
      Sacramental Orders, Lex Orandi Series (Collegeville, Minn: Liturgical
      Press, 2000), chapter 1.
20.   Schillebeeckx, *The Church with a Human Face*, 205.

2. *Communio* and the array of ministries

The documents of the Second Vatican Council contain a range of images and concepts that express the nature of the church and its mission, among them: the people of God, the body of Christ, and the sacrament of salvation. However it has been widely recognised by theologians and the magisterium that the concept of the church as *communio* is pivotal to the council's interpretation of these other understandings of the church. [21] In its final report, the 1985 Synod of Bishops acknowledges the significance of this concept for the council: 'The ecclesiology of communion is the central and fundamental idea of the council's documents'. [22]

Speaking of the church as *communio* certainly brings the gathered community to the fore, yet the heart of the meaning of *communio* is in the action of God. The communion of the church is brought about by the Spirit at work in the witness of the apostolic group. As J-M R Tillard puts it, the church as communion is composed of three integral, entwined elements: 'the Spirit, the apostolic witness which centres on the Lord Jesus Christ, and the *communion* in which the human multitude and its diversity are contained within this unity and where the unity is expressed in the multitude and its diversity'. [23] As communion, therefore, the church expresses the mystery of God at work in the world: it is the 'sign of trinitarian *communion* in the fraternal relationships among the disciples of Christ'. [24]

Within this symphony of communion, ministry plays an essential part. Ordained ministers interpret and hand on the apostolic word, and for this reason Tillard sees them as at the service of communion. As he puts it, these servants of the church of God are introduced into the communion of the apostles, 'so that the church remains within the dynamism of what the Spirit has 'delivered' by them (*paradosis*),

---

21. See Walter Kasper, '*Communio*: The Guiding Concept of Catholic Ecumenical Theology', *That They May All Be One*, 58; J-M R Tillard, *Church of Churches: The Ecclesiology of Communion*, translated by RC De Peaux (Collegeville, Minn: Liturgical Press, 1992).

22. Extraordinary Synod Bishops, 'The Final Report', *Origins* 15/27 (December 1985): 444–50 at 448 (II C 1).

23. Tillard, *Church of Churches*, 8.

24. Tillard, *Church of Churches*, 51.

always faithful to the deposit of faith (*parathèkè*) and obedient to what it implies'.[25]

Most significant for my purposes in this understanding of the church adopted by Vatican II is the essential relationship envisaged between the ordained ministry and the ministry of the baptised. I have already pointed out that this relationship had been lost from sight for at least a millennium prior to the council.[26] Yet the early Christian community was keenly aware of the Spirit calling the entire people of God to the service of the gospel. Included in a list of services of the gospel from the Pauline letters and the Acts of the Apostles, drawn up by Tillard, are prophecy, instruction, explaining the Good News, refuting error, and many more. The communion of the early community came into being through this wide range of services of the gospel, which the leaders of the community were called to recognise. William Harmless's study of the catechumenate during Augustine's life and ministry (354–430) describes the rich variety of ministries in which both ordained and non-ordained were engaged.[27] In Augustine's catechumenate, lay teachers and catechists had an official role in the liturgical life and were seen as graced instruments. When the church is understood in terms of *communio*, ordained ministers have a significant role, but are not the source of all ministries. In Tillard's view, ordained ministers have a directive role in the communion, yet every initiative in the service of the gospel does not depend on them.[28]

3. The ministry of women

From the above I hope that it is clear that the question of the ordination of women is raised in a fundamentally new context on two fronts following the Second Vatican Council. Any faithful response to this question now must recognise the equal and unique dignity of women. And secondly, the question is raised in a context in which the role of

---

25.   Tillard, *Church of Churches*, 183.
26.   Tillard makes the same point about the clergy absorbing and monopolising roles meant for the whole of the community. See Tillard, *Church of Churches*, 211–15.
27.   William Harmless, *Augustine and the Catechumenate* (Collegeville, Minn.: Liturgical Press, 1995).
28.   Tillard, *Church of Churches*, 214.

the ordained ministry can no longer absorb and monopolise the ministry of the whole community, but rather bring to fruition a vast range of ministries at the service of the gospel. This is an immense challenge on which we have only just embarked.

In *Ordinatio Sacerdotalis*, published in 1994, Pope John Paul II reiterated the teaching of the Congregation for the Doctrine of the Faith that the church 'does not consider herself authorised to admit women to priestly ordination'.[29] Because this teaching 'has been preserved by the constant and universal Tradition of the Church and firmly taught by the Magisterium', Pope John Paul II concludes that it must 'be definitively held by all the Church's faithful'.[30] In the following year the Prefect of the Congregation for the Doctrine of the Faith, the then Cardinal Ratzinger, responding to discussion within the theological community about the level of authority in *Ordinatio Sacerdotalis*, confirmed that 'this teaching requires definitive assent, since, founded on the written word of God and from the beginning constantly preserved and applied in the tradition of the Church, it has been set forth infallibly by the ordinary and universal magisterium'.[31] According to the Second Vatican Council's document on the church, *Lumen Gentium*, the response due to the Pope's authentic teaching from all the church's faithful including theologians is 'religious assent of will and intellect'.[32] The assent envisaged in *Lumen Gentium* is one in which believers allow the truth of the teaching to penetrate their whole lives. This understanding is beautifully reflected in the response of

---

29. Pope John Paul II, *On Reserving Priestly Ordination to Men Alone* (Homebush, NSW: St Pauls, 1994), n 2. Here the pope quotes: Congregation for the Doctrine of the Faith, *Inter Insignores*, in *Origins* 6/33, n 100.

30. Pope John Paul II, *On Reserving Priestly Ordination*, n 4.

31. Congregation for the Doctrine of the Faith, 'Reply to the "Dubium" Concerning the Doctrine Contained in the Apostolic Letter "Ordinatio Sacerdotalis"', in *From 'Inter Insignores' to 'Ordinatio Sacerdoatlis': Documents and Commentaries* (Washington, DC: United States Catholic Conference, 1998), 197.

32. Second Vatican Council, *Lumen Gentium*, n 25 (Tanner translation). For a full discussion of this issue as it applies to Catholic theologians, see John M Huels, 'The Juridic Status of Catholic Faculties of Theology: Overview of the Universal Law,' *Studia Canonica* 37 (2003): 301–22, particularly 317–8.

Pedro Arrupe, Jesuit Superior General at the time, to the publication of *Humanae Vitae*:

> Every Jesuit owes it to himself, by reason of his vocation to do everything possible to penetrate, and to help others penetrate, into a thought which may not have been his own previously . . . To obey therefore, is not to stop thinking; to parrot the encyclical word for word in a servile manner. On the contrary, it is to commit oneself to study it as profoundly as possible so as to discover for oneself and to show others the meaning of an intervention judged necessary by the Holy Father.[33]

In dealing with this papal teaching, I believe that the Roman Catholic Church must embrace it and at the same time embrace a realistic and viable commitment to recognise women's equality in their role in the church. A significant step in this direction has been taken here in the Archdiocese of Adelaide. In 1986 my predecessor Archbishop Leonard Faulkner appointed a *Diocesan Pastoral Team*, comprising a lay and a religious woman as well as a priest, to assist him in the governance of the Archdiocese. After my installation as Archbishop I appointed the two women incumbents as *Chancellors of Mission* and *Stewardship* for the Archdiocese and in that way recognised their ministry within the mainstream of the church's life by giving it a canonical place. In cooperation with me, these women participate equally at the most senior level of leadership in the Archdiocese of Adelaide. Over the years the women who have occupied these positions have offered invaluable leadership, which has been a great source of renewal in faith for the Archdiocese. In making these appointments, my intention has been to accept the church's teaching about reserving ordination to men and to move ahead on the significant issues of the equality of women in the church, and developing the integral relationship between ordained ministry and

---

33. Pedro Arrupe, SJ, *Epistula ARPN Generalis ad Omnen Societatem Occasione Litterarum Encyclicarum 'Humanae Vitae'*, Acta Romana Societas Iesu, vol xv, Fasciculus II, Anno 1968.

the ministry of all the baptised. This is one step—yet a significant one—in our commitment to the equality of women in the church and to fostering the service of the gospel in the communion

Living Trinitarian Faith: A Restructured Theology of the Ordained Ministry

Josephine Armour OP
Adelaide

It is remarkable that in this early period of the twenty-first century we still debate the issue of the ordination of women to the public ministry of the church. Over thirty years ago, the great Catholic theologian, Karl Rahner, reflected on this question and concluded, 'I see no reason in principle to give a negative answer to this question'.[1] Rahner himself would perhaps be surprised to learn that the ordination of women has still not come to fruition in the Roman Catholic Church. Why is this? It is not my intention to refute again the oft-critiqued arguments put forward to rationalise the exclusion of women from the public ministry of the church. Rather, I believe that in order to reach resolution in this debate we must review the very theology that underpins our understanding of ministry.

Before her untimely death Catherine LaCugna argued in her book, *God For Us*, that the doctrine of the Trinity suggests to us ways of living our Christian life in communion with one another. Since the church purports to be the people of God the church ought to manifest the nature of God. We ought to *live* trinitarian faith, to *be* the visible sign of God's reign, to embody the presence of God in our world. LaCugna writes,

> The doctrine of the Trinity is ultimately a teaching not about the abstract nature of God, nor about God in isolation from everything other than God, but a teaching about God's life with us and our life with each other.[2]

---

1.   Karl Rahner, *The Shape of the Church to Come* (New York: Seabury Press, 1974), 114.

2.   Catherine Mowry LaCugna, *God For Us: the Trinity and Christian Life* (San Francisco: Harper, 1991), 1.

I am taking up Catherine LaCugna's challenge to the church and proposing a theology of the ordained ministry that is based upon the symbol of the Trinity. Because the doctrine of the Trinity is a teaching about God's life with us, it can provide us with a framework for understanding ordained ministry in the context of all ministry in the Christian community. It will be shown that this framework in no way restricts ordination to males, but rather insists upon a diverse and inclusive ministry in which women have an equal and vital role.

What do we know about the life and nature of God?
LaCugna and other scholars before her have expressed the nature of the Trinity as God existing as three persons in mutual and loving relationship and oriented in relationship to the whole of creation. LaCugna writes, 'The Trinity overflows to include humanity as its beloved partners'.[3]

The doctrine of the Trinity reveals a God who is essentially relational, who is three persons united in radical communion, who is non-hierarchical, whose authority is grounded in the *koinonia* of the three persons, whose mutual love between three persons overflows to all creation, and who calls forth loving relationships in the Christian community. Where better to look for an image or framework for Christian ministry than the very life of God. Ministry in the Christian community, as much as is humanly possible, ideally can embody or give expression to the life of the triune God.[4] La Cugna suggests that

> we may ask whether our institutions, rituals and administrative practices foster elitism, discrimination, competition, . . . or whether the church is run like God's household: a domain of inclusiveness, inter-dependence, and co-operation, structures according to the model of *perichoresis* among persons.[5]

The doctrine of the Trinity provides a critical principle against which we can evaluate present practices in ministry, such as the exclusion of women from the ordained ministry, and it can be an agent

---

3.   *Ibid.*
4.   I define ministry as the public activity of a baptized follower of Jesus Christ. It is carried out on behalf of the Christian community for the purposes of building up and nourishing the people of God.
5.   LaCugna, *God For Us*, 402.

of change, attuning us to the life of God. How would Christian ministry operate if it were based upon the very life of God?

1. Ministry: an expression of the God who is three persons in mutual relationship

The ministry of the church, which must be understood in the context of the Christian community, ought to manifest the mutual and equal relations that are disclosed in the triune God. The nature of the triune God affirms that right relationships within the Christian community and with the wider world ought to be highly valued and nurtured. The nature of the Trinity affirms the notion that the ministry of the church ought to be grounded in the *koinonia* of the Christian community, that is, in the essential relatedness or the bond of discipleship in the community.

1.1 The people of God as community

In spite of the divisions within the church that damage the cause of the gospel, the Christian community, in so far as it is in Christ, is radically one. Christians are called to a genuine community in which right relationship is embodied.

The very nature of God is revealed to us through the person of Jesus Christ in the power of the Holy Spirit. All baptised Christians, women and men, are therefore called to participate in God's life by standing *in persona Christi*, acting as Christ to others, through the inspiration of the Spirit. Traditionally, the Roman Catholic Church has attributed this representational function solely to the ordained minister, when it properly belongs to all of the baptized. It is the way of Christian discipleship. For this reason, this fundamental mode of relating, that of standing *in persona Christi* to one another, is also fundamental to all ministry. All ministry is grounded in this call of baptism.

1.2 The relationship between the ordained ministry and the
Christian community

The ordained ministry, as a particular dimension of the church's ministry, has a distinct and essential relationship to the Christian community. Edward Schillebeeckx has noted that discussions about the meaning and function of the ordained minister traditionally have been far too centred upon the ontological character of the ordained person and too little concerned with the relationship of that person with the Christian community.[6]

If we shift our attention from the question of the ontological character of the minister to the relationship between the minister and the community, it is clear that ordination has no meaning outside of the Christian community. The situation which has arisen today where ordained men travel across the world to work in other communities which are supposedly without ministers ought to be viewed as an anomaly. Ordained ministers ought more properly serve the local community in which their ministry arose. However, the requirement of the current magisterium of the Roman Catholic Church that this ministry be confined to celibate males, has given rise to an apparent paucity of ministers. Local communities, open to the Spirit of God, do give birth to ministers. There is no shortage of ministers. The Spirit of God does inspire and raise up leaders and ministers if we are only open to that fact. Often those ministers will be married people and often they will be women.

The ministry of the church ought to give expression to the relationality of the triune God. Ministry in the local community ought to be shared and collaborative, rather than lodged in the hands of one person.

The ordained ministry, in particular, sanctioned and affirmed by the one church, serves to connect and unify the peoples, communities and nations who are represented by all ministers. The distinguishing feature of the ordained ministry is its role of representing the one, holy, catholic and apostolic church, a role that maintains and consolidates both the unity and diversity of the church. That role is a symbolic one. Nevertheless, the practical functions of ministry are many and cannot be left to ordained ministers alone, but rather to all of those who are called and gifted in pastoral work. This is, of course, happening already in many places today, although the ministry of those not ordained is often not fully acknowledged.

2. Ministry: manifesting the non-hierarchical nature of God

A number of scholars including Elizabeth Johnson, Catherine LaCugna, and Miroslav Volf show that the Trinity is non-hierarchical.[7]

---

6. Edward Schillebeeckx, *The Church with a Human Face: a New and Expanded Theology of Ministry* (New York: Crossroad, 1992), 205ff.

For LaCugna, God is the three divine persons, who 'mutually inhere in one another, draw life from one another, and "are" what they are by relation to one another'.[8] The icon of the Trinity actually critiques ways of relating that give elevated status to any role in the community, since its very life honours the equality, mutuality and distinctiveness of three persons united in the One God. 'Trinitarian communion is opposed to hierarchicalism in the church.'[9] In the Trinity, there is no basis for domination or power over others. The ministry of the church, then, can mirror these qualities and be collaborative, non-hierarchical and involve both women and men, married or celibate. The mutuality and equality of the persons of the Trinity affirms the claim that the relationships amongst ordained ministers, and between ordained ministers and the rest of the baptised can be collegial, collaborative and offer mutual service to one another. In a collaborative ministry, the interaction between ministers and the community is highly valued and responsibility shared.

The insights of feminist theologians offer a variety of models for understanding the office of the church that are essentially non-hierarchical and collaborative. Lynn Rhodes suggests that we can view ministry by using images of friendship. In her thinking, the church itself is a community of friends who are independent, mutually caring and accountable to one another.

> [F]riendship suggests both the emotional intimacy we need and the mutuality, nurture, trust and accountability that we value. The most powerful and best friendships we have give us insight into love that implies reciprocity and an authority of selfhood that neither demands the other's acquiescence nor makes the self subservient. It does not deny uniqueness nor does it require hierarchy in order to be functional.[10]

---

7. See Elizabeth Johnson, *She Who Is* (New York: Crossoad, 1994), 194–197, LaCugna, *God For Us*, 270–278, and Miroslav Volf, *After Our Likeness: the Church as the Image of the Trinity* (Grand Rapids: Eerdmans, 1998), 214–220.
8. La Cugna, *God For Us*, 270–21.
9. *Ibid*, 278.
10. Anne Rhodes, *Co-creating: a Feminist View of Ministry* (Philadelphia: Westminster, 1987), 123.

Rhodes's model for ministry is consonant with the paradigm of the perichoretic love of the triune God. No persons have particular power or authority over another, but rather respond to one another mutually.

A collaborative form of ministry influences the ways in which those in the community relate to one another. Given an understanding of the triune God as inherently relational, an appropriate way of relating in Christian communities is by conversation that is characterised by deep connection, co-operation and mutuality. We might seek conversation that is not didactic but empathetic, non-judgmental, receptive, passionate, honest and self-disclosing.[11]

Both women and men need to be involved in ministry, but what is more important is the way in which that ministry is conducted. The mode of operation in ministry must be collaborative and non-hierarchical. If ministry is to be truly collaborative it is important that there is a mutuality in exchanges between those who minister and those who receive ministrations. It is important that ministers are able to receive ministrations from others. All of the baptised, whether ordained or not, may at different times be engaged in both giving and receiving ministrations. This means that there may not be strict divisions between those who learn and those who teach, or those who serve and those who are served.

Rosemary Ruether's proposal for a non-hierarchical ministry envisions a community of 'enablers'.[12] Since no one person has all the skills to satisfy the needs of the community, she rightly argues that the community itself must look among its ranks for those with gifts. These people, women and men, will be empowered to use their talents and to nurture the talents of others.

In collaborative styles of ministry, authority ought not to be located in one person, over and against others, but can rather be invested in the bonds of relationship between the baptised faithful. This is not to say that there is no place for episcopal leadership. It is to suggest that the bishop's role of oversight and leadership ought not to be an authoritarian one, but one that involves collaboration with the people of God to hold together and protect the diversity of local communities. This task involves the nurturing of links between local communities, and between the universal church and local communities. It demands a

---

11.   *Ibid.*
12.   Rosemary Ruether, *Women—Church: Theology and Practice* (San Francisco: Harper, 1988), 89–90.

respect for the authority of discernment processes which involve the representation of views from the whole of the believing community. It is through the episcopacy that the unity of local communities is made manifest. This role is not without tension since the very diversity of communities can give rise to variations in values, religious practices and theological understandings. Cultural practices which may have a long history in a local community may need to be woven into the practices of the church in the local context.[13] The question as to whether the exclusion of women from the ordained ministry of the church is indeed part of cultural practice in much of our world is one which must be asked. The church must preserve the essence of the apostolic tradition but continually engage in necessarily critical inquiry, which is the work of theology. It is the bishop who bears a particular responsibility for the preservation of the apostolic tradition and who yet must be open to and encouraging of critical reflection upon the tradition and to the ongoing revelation of God in the world. This perhaps irresolvable tension must be held by the bishops as part of the responsibility of *episcope* or oversight.

The *koinonia* of the three persons of the Trinity extends beyond the inner life of God to involve the people of God. Therefore the work of decision-making and administration of the church must be conducted collaboratively and collegially, centred in the *koinonia* of all the baptised people of God, both ordained and non-ordained, both women and men. The baptised people of God must be involved in the decision-making procedures of the church through representatives who attend gatherings, councils or synods in which decisions are made.

---

13. This interweaving of local religious customs and universal liturgical practices contributes to the diversity of communities. For example, some indigenous North American Catholic communities have incorporated the traditional practice of smudging into the Eucharistic celebration, a practice which enhances and furthers the notion of blessing present in the Catholic tradition. Other local communities have local concerns: for example, the people living at the base of the dormant Mt Vesuvius call upon the locally revered St Gennaro for protection from harm when the volcano erupts. Universalising such local customs would be absurd, and yet the significance of local custom for the local community deserves protection.

3. Ministry: a focus of the unity and diversity of God

The ministry of the Roman Catholic Church, and its ordained ministry in particular, ought to manifest both unity and diversity. The implications of this claim are that the ministry should include people of many cultures and classes, women as well as men, both celibate and those not vowed to a celibate life-style.

Ordination is bestowed upon those ministers of the church who have the distinctive symbolic task of maintaining the unity or connectedness as well as the diversity of the Christian church. This is ideally accomplished when the ordained minister arises from and is affirmed as a leader in the local community and is therefore able to represent the diverse local community to the universal church and to represent the universal church to the local community. The doctrine of the Trinity affirms that the three persons of the Trinity are diverse, but also united in mutual love. The diversity and distinctiveness of the three is held in tension with the essential oneness of God. This quality of diversity within unity provides a foundation for understanding the ministry of the church also as diverse but essentially one.

There is only one ministry of the Christian church originating in the person and work of Jesus of Nazareth and ongoing through the power of the Spirit of God. Nevertheless this ministry is ideally as diverse as the gifts given to the baptised members of the church. Furthermore, the ministry of the church is not and cannot be contained within the ordained ministry. The interaction of many, diverse ministries in the church gives form to the variety of gifts empowered by the Spirit.

Miroslav Volf has good grounds for arguing that the church was founded through the presence of Christ in the Holy Spirit and 'is constituted by way of the entire called and charismatically endowed people of God'.[14] This is how Christ acts in our world today: through the gifts of the Spirit that are bestowed not only upon the ordained but upon all of the baptised.

> This is why a division into those who serve in the congregation and those who are served is ecclesiologically unacceptable; every person is to serve with his or her specific gifts and every person is to be served in his or her specific need.[15]

---

14. Volf, *After Our Likeness*, 228.
15. *Ibid*, 230.

I am not suggesting that all of the baptised are ministers, but rather that the gifts of ministry are so dispersed amongst the baptised that the work of ministry cannot be contained within the ordained ministry. A concrete example of ministerial gifts bestowed both in and beyond the ordained ministry is the ministry of prophecy that often arises where it is least expected. It cannot be contained in the ordained ministry. The ministry of the church must include the work of ordained and unordained ministers. The one ministry is fundamentally diverse and cannot be understood as contained within an all-male celibate priesthood.

Furthermore, the ordained ministry itself ought to be understood as diverse within its unity and ought to reflect the diversity of the Christian community from which it arises. Since its specific distinguishing role is the representation of the local church to the universal church and conversely the representation of the universal church to the local community, the ordained ministry must adequately reflect the diversity of the people whom it is representing. In this way, the ordained ministry maintains and consolidates the unity and diversity of the church. As already stated above, it must include people of many races, cultures and classes, women as well as men, and both celibate people and those not vowed to a celibate life-style.

Anne Carr suggests a much more inclusive policy in the ordaining of ministers:

> Because it [ordained ministry] would include in its pastoral, liturgical and social expressions a full representation of classes, races, and sexes, it would witness to its belief in 'neither Greek nor Jew, slave nor free, male nor female.' ... The mutual involvement of men and women in the sacramental ministry would be an intrinsic sign of the service of unity required by the gospel.[16]

It is important that all ministries of the church have an explicit sacramental dimension. Since it is already the case that women as well as men are involved in the pastoral ministry of the church it is not

---

16.   Anne Carr, *Transforming Grace: Christian Tradition and Women's Experience* (San Francisco: Harper and Row, 1988), 38–9.

appropriate that women be excluded in principle from the ordained ministry. As Carr again explains,

> As long as women are barred from full recognition and sacramental completion of the service they are already fulfilling . . . the language of the church is unfortunately clear in what it is saying to women and to the world about women.[17]

Alternatively, if women were to be included amongst the ordained, the diversity of the ministry is more fully acknowledged both sacramentally and practically.

In honouring its diversity, the ordained ministry must also include those who have not undertaken a celibate life-style. Those who come to the ministry of the church from experiences of Christian marriage, partnership, sexual engagement, child-bearing and child rearing bring to that ministry, depths of understanding human experience that cannot be present in a solely masculine and celibate ministry. That is not to say that all ministers need to have experienced the whole gamut of possibilities to be of pastoral worth, but the wholesale exclusion from the ministry of people other than celibate males is unacceptable.

The ordained ministry ought to reflect the diversity of culture that exists amongst the baptised people of God. This ought to involve openness to the needs of various cultures and national groups and openness to cultural variations in liturgical practice and customs. These various ways of expressing the one faith deserve to be celebrated for they add to the richness of the universal church.

An opening of the ordained ministry to a greater diversity of ministers will result in expansion of the ordained ministry. An expansion of the ordained ministry would have the advantage of providing a larger and more diverse group of people who would preside at the eucharist in local communities, also enabling ordained persons to engage in a greater variety of pastoral, prophetic and educational tasks. This would alleviate the narrowing of the tasks of the ordained into the liturgical functions. It may arise that in any one parish or community there are two or three ordained persons who engage in a variety of ministerial tasks, one of which is presiding at the eucharist. In summary, the ministry ought to be both diverse but one,

---

17.   *Ibid*, 39.

manifesting the nature of God as three diverse persons united in the one God.

4. Ministry: manifesting the ecstasy of God

The triune God does not remain apart from the whole of creation but is so related to all that is, that all of creation is caught up in the life of God. LaCugna explains, 'God goes forth from God, God creates the world, God suffuses its history and dwells within us, redeeming the world from within'.[18] She continues, 'There is no rest (*stasis*) in *ekstasis*, only continual movement outward'.[19] The life of God shows forth mutual and just relationships and continually reaches outward to embrace all of creation, inviting the wider society to a loving, mutual and just way of being. Wherever there are distorted relationships, whether between people, races, sexes or between the human community and the rest of creation, the life of the Trinity acts to challenge them. Where there are relationships of domination and subjection, or of abuse, the life of the Trinity stands as a critique in its revelation of radical relationality and mutual love.

The ministry of the church and the ordained ministry in particular, in manifesting the ecstatic life of God, can similarly be caught up in the life of the community and call the wider society to a loving, mutual and just way of being. It needs also to be open to the call of the wider society to it, for right relationship.

The work of Christian ministry, if it is to embody the life of God, will reach out beyond itself. It will both affect and be affected by the wider community of which it is a part. Christian ministry must hold in tension its own openness to the diversity of the human community and a vision for the fullness of humanity. The role of Christian ministers within the community might be to challenge but never to dominate or coerce others toward a particular point of view. Christian ministry will influence and be influenced by others when it strives to establish equal and mutual relationships in which each party grows in its sense of identity and personhood. In manifesting the ecstatic nature of the triune God, ordained Christian ministers, who represent the church, neither lose their own unique sense of purpose nor subjugate others. The diversity and differences amongst the human community become a resource for human learning to be celebrated and protected. In this

---

18. LaCugna, *God For Us*, 353.
19. *Ibid*, 351.

movement beyond itself, the Christian church is called to greater ecumenism. If each denominational church, including the Roman Catholic Church, is to be open to renewal and change, it will be important to acknowledge the work of the Spirit in other Christian denominations, recognising not only Christian baptism in each church but also other forms of Christian ministry. The Christian churches are invited by the Spirit to give concrete form to the unity and communion that is at the heart of Christianity. As Schillebeeckx rightly argues, 'The scandal is not that there are differences [between the Christian churches] but that these differences are used as an obstacle to communion'.[20]

It is because the very life of God reveals mutual, loving and just relationship that God can call forth the same from the people of God. How important it is, then, that the leadership of the church together with the baptised, embody such right relationship amongst themselves. If mutual and just relationships are not present in the life of the church, then the church lacks credibility in calling for right relationships in the wider society. It is the embodiment of God's way of being amongst the community that will have ecstatic affect. The manifestation of God's life by the baptised cannot help but extend beyond itself, calling forth right relationships amongst all beings.

When the ministry of the church, and the ordained ministry in particular, is caught up in the life of the community and when it calls the wider society to a loving, mutual and just way of being, it acts prophetically. It is oriented towards the hope of the future and towards a vision of what might be. It is exemplified in Schillebeeckx's discussions of the negative experiences of contrast in which people resist the suffering and oppression in our world because they know at the depths of their being that there is a possibility of a better world. Schillebeeckx argues that all people, Christians and agnostics alike, share this experience of 'openness to the unknown and the better'.[21]

5. The need for the democratisation of the church

Since the triune God is three persons in mutual relationship and is non-hierarchical in structure, there are good grounds for suggesting that the ministry of the church and the ordained ministry in particular, ought to be structured non-hierarchically and in a way that promotes

---

20. Schillebeeckx, *Church*, 197.
21. *Ibid*, 5,6.

collegiality and collaboration amongst the baptised people of God. However, a more collaborative form of ministry as I have described can only emerge if the church embraces democratisation. The democratisation of the church ought not to be feared but rather viewed as a way of being open to God's ways.

I have offered here a vision of ordained ministry that is grounded in the context of the mission and ministry of the universal church. The ordained ministry must embody as much as is humanly possible, the life of the triune God. It must be a ministry based on a mutual and just relationship between all persons, and though there is only one ministry, it must embody the diversity of the Christian community. The ordained ministry must therefore work to maintain and consolidate both the unity and the diversity of the Christian church. Finally, it must be non-hierarchical and embody the ecstatic nature of God. That is, it must move beyond itself, for the fullness of relationship.

Women and Ministry in the Light of 'Who Touched Me' (Luke 8:45)

John Collins
Melbourne

First-world women have achieved much since Mary Wollstonecraft claimed in 1792 that 'reason . . . demands justice for one-half of the human race.'[1] One hundred and one years later women in New Zealand were the first of that half of the race to vote in a national election. Precisely 200 years later, in November 1992, the General Synod of the Church of England passed by a two-thirds majority 'the Priests (Ordination of Women) Measure'. The thumping vote was this church's answer to the question put by one of the speakers in synodal debate: '[A]re the gifts which God has given to women acceptable in his service in the office of priest?'[2]

Two years after this, and marking the end of twenty years' public debate in the course of which the Pontifical Biblical Commission of the Roman Catholic Church discerned no obstacle in the Scriptures to the ordination of women,[3] Pope John Paul II passed his judgment on the issue—which was to be held 'definitively by all'—that 'the church has no authority whatsoever to confer priestly ordination on women'.[4] The grounds for the judgment are well known. In Christian Duquoc's summary, these were 'the silence of Jesus, his maleness, the decision of the first Christians to exclude women from church government and

---

1. *A Vindication of the Rights of Woman*, edited by Miriam Brody (London: Penguin 1992), 89.
2. David McLean in *The Ordination of Women to the Priesthood: the Synod Debate 11 November 1992: The Verbatim Record* (London: Church House 1993), 47.
3. 'Biblical Commission Report Can Women Be Priests?', in *Women Priests: A Catholic Commentary on the Vatican Declaration*, edited by Leonard Swidler and Arlene Swidler (New York: Paulist 1977), 338–46; see there also John R Donahue, 'A Tale of Two Documents', 25–34.
4. Apostolic Letter of John Paul II, *On Reserving Priestly Ordination to Men Alone* (Homebush, NSW: St Pauls 1994), paragraph 4.

priesthood'. But Duquoc also noted how the Catholic community found itself 'constrained to use doubtful anthropological reasons to justify its historical antipathy to giving women sacramental and hierarchical responsibility'.[5] So disabling did Duquoc judge this 'attachment to earlier forms and decisions[6] that he weighed it against the church's overriding responsibility to the word of God. This was the word which brought into being a 'sisterhood and brotherhood' as 'a symbolic anticipation of the kingdom of God'.[7] Such a word ensures an originating and ongoing equality that requires access of women to roles assumed by the hierarchy.

1. Ministry of the word

Duquoc's trajectory here is of great interest to me in that it parallels the outcomes of a critical review of the nature of first Christian ministry in my area of research.[8] Here, instead of ministry being viewed primarily—as happens in the Roman Catholic tradition—within a theology of sacraments, where it functions as an agency of sacramentality, ministry itself becomes the purveyor of the mysterious but revealing and enlightening word of God. This ministry is authoritative both by reason of the word it has received and by reason of the ecclesial mandate which constitutes the function precisely as a ministry. Its essentially ecclesial character is evidenced in its outcome, namely, that believers have first become susceptible to the allure of the divine invitation issuing from the word and have then, once possessed of the word, become partners in dialogue with the word, experiencing its authority, mystery, and power. As believers, each perceives that she or he is one of many and that there is now 'neither male nor female' but all are as 'one in Christ' (Gal 3:28–29), and are thus the assembly, *ekklesia*, of those whom God has called.[9]

---

5.   *Provisional Churches*, English translation (London: SCM 1986), 93
6.   *Provisional Churches*, 92.
7.   *Provisional Churches*, 101-03.
8.   Principally my *Diakonia: Re-interpreting the Ancient Sources* (New York: Oxford University Press 1990); *Are All Christians Ministers?* (Collegeville, MN: Liturgical Press 1992); 'The Mediatorial Aspect of Paul's Role as *Diakonos*', *Australian Biblical Review* 40(1992): 34–44; 'A Ministry for Tomorrow's Church', *Journal of Ecumenical Studies* 32/2 (Spring 1995): 159–78.
9.   Compare the definition of the church in *Catechism of the Catholic Church*, number 777.

This is the reality of ministry and *ekklesia* as expounded by Paul when defending the authenticity of his own apostleship in 2 Corinthians 3–6. That Paul conducted the apologia throughout not in terms of apostleship but in terms of *diakonia*—the Greek word that after the manner of the Latin bible we translate as 'ministry'—has much to say to the church today about how intimately the word of God is at play within the Body of Christ. Paul turned from the technical term 'apostleship' to the non-technical term *diakonia* for two reasons. The first of these is precisely the technicality of apostleship, that is, the paper credentials from distant authorities establishing the *bona fides* of the apostle. But, as Paul says, that is just paper. Accordingly, he had reason to choose a different course, and this was to ask the jury, namely, his Corinthian audience, to assess the authenticity of his work among them by the effects they had experienced from it. Whether as apostleship or as *diakonia*/ministry, Paul's work was to deliver the word of God. But by designating this work *diakonia* Paul was turning away from mere paper formalities to the rhetoric of philosophers that allowed him and his audience to reflect on the actual religious experience—their very 'consciousness' (*syneidesis*, 2 Cor 4:2)—of encountering the word of God.

We can appreciate the rhetorical impact of this by glancing at how some Hellenistic writers expressed processes of mediation. Thus, in explaining translucence, Alexander of Aphrodisias noted that, though colourless, air and water let the colours of other things pass through them; they are thus 'conductive' elements (*diakonos, de Mixtione* 5.14). (We recall that Paul named himself and Apollos 'ministers [*diakonoi*] through whom you believed' [1 Cor 3:5]: Paul and Apollos had received the word from God and passed it on to the believing Corinthians.) The Aristotelian philosopher Themistius pointed out (in *De anima* 125.9) that in our seeing, hearing and smelling we are not in direct contact with objects as we are when we touch things but receive these other sensory impressions by virtue of some other object (the air) acting 'as a medium in between' (*metaxu diakonountos*) us and the sensed object.[10] The purpose of Paul's similar rhetoric is to expose the process of apostleship as one that mediates mystery from one divine sphere to another human sphere. In coming to realise that they had been involved in such a heart-touching experience—having received a

---

10. See other illustrations of the usage in 'The Mediatorial Aspect' (preceding note).

word 'written . . . on human hearts' (2 Cor 3:3)—the Corinthians
cannot fail to recognise in Paul the authentic apostle. Paul certainly
labours the point, culminating in identifying his work as 'the
diakonia/ministry of reconciliation' (2 Cor 5:18). This English expression
(RSV) lacks the staggering immediacy of Paul's Greek as understood
by William Tyndale in translating it as 'the preaching of the
atonement', where we are to understand an 'at-one-ment' between the
benevolent deity and 'the new creation'.[11]

2. Taking the bypass

Such a theology of the ministry of the word exposes the common
ground on which women and men stand in their communion with the
divine. Neither has a greater proficiency or precedence over the other
in this communion, but each rather enriches the other in that very
communion. Put simply, does a woman not hear, become attracted to,
receive and embrace the word of God as eagerly or warmly as a man?
And can a woman not purvey this word as effectively as a man? The
answers to these crucial questions are immediately clear, and woman's
capacity for ministry/*diakonia* is thereby immediately established and
recognisable. On this ground alone I believe we are able to press on
effectively and inevitably to the attainment of that justice for women
that Mary Wollstonecraft demanded. In the process we would have the
significant advantage of being able to bypass several other well-worn
approaches to outstanding problems of women in the churches, in
particular their access to leading ecclesial roles.

Among these approaches the search for precedents in the
ordination of women has been prominent,[12] but remains inconclusive
and ineffectual.[13] Questionable also is any demand by women for

---

11. *Tyndale's New Testament* [1534], edited by David Daniell (New Haven:
     Yale, 1989).
12. As in the publicity attracted by Mary Anne Rossi's account of research
     by Giorgio Otranto, 'Note sul sacerdozio femminile nell'antichità',
     Vetera Christianorum 19(1982): 341–60. Thus, Carolyn Moynihan
     Bradt, 'Evidence Exists: Women Were Priests and Bishops in the First
     Five Centuries of the Church', *New Women, New Church* 13/2–4 (May-
     October 1990): 1 and 4. Further documentation at http://www.women
     priests.org/traditio/otran_1.asp. Rossi published an English translation in
     Journal of Feminist Studies in Religion 7/2(Spring, 1991).
13. Largely because more is made of the evidence than it can bear, as in
     Karen Jo Torjesen, *When Women Were Priests: Women's Leadership in*

entry into a sacerdotal priesthood, although much excitement attended the belated discovery of the secret priestly ordination in Prague of Ludmila Javorova and her peers by Bishop Felix Davidek in 1970.[14] At the same time strong differences of opinion among women emerged about the appropriateness of women's ordinations by dissident bishops.[15] In fact, many women themselves reject priestly ordination as an objective because such a step would simply replicate the clerical sacerdotalism whose pastoral inadequacies they have closely observed in the post-conciliar struggle between parties favouring on the one hand a reformed presbyterate and, on the other, a restored priesthood.[16] Hence, groups advocating women's ordination often do so under a protocol like that of the Australian OCW (Ordination of Catholic Women), 'Action for the ordination of catholic women into a renewed priestly ministry'.[17]

---

the Early Church and the Scandal of their Subordination in the Rise of Christianity (San Francisco: Harper, 1993). Such criticism cannot be directed against Ute E Eisen, *Amtsträgerinnen im frühen Christentum* (Göttingen: Vandenhoeck & Ruprecht, 1996), although the evidence remains minor and perhaps ambiguous; see my 'Ute Eisen on Early Women Office-Bearers', *Women-Church* 26 (Autumn 2000): 38–42.

14. Miriam Therese Winter, *Out of the Depths: The Story of Ludmila Javorova Ordained Roman Catholic Priest* (New York: Crossroad, 2001).

15. See reports at http://www.catholicnewtimes.org/ (25 January 2004), and discussion at http://www.catholicnewtimes.org/.

16. These tensions pervade conventional theologies of priesthood like those of Jean Galot, *Theology of the Priesthood*, English translation (San Francisco: Ignatius Press, 1985) and Gustave Martelet, *Théologie du sacerdoce* (Paris: Cerf, 1990). Edward Schillebeeckx has noted the compromise attempted at the Second Vatican Council in *The Church with a Human Face*, English trans (London: SCM, 1985), 203, and proceeded to trace the tensions in the subsequent Roman Synod on the priesthood of 1971 (211–36), pointing out more than once that the deliberations 'did not match up with pastoral demands' (226). Addressing the tensions at the opening of the Synod on formation for the priesthood in 1990, Joseph Ratzinger bemoaned the abandonment of 'the ancient conceptions of cult and priesthood' while arguing for their reinstatement; see 'On the Essence of the Priesthood' in his *Called to Communion*, English translation (San Francisco: Ignatius, 1996), 105–31 (citation, 109).

17. *OCW News*, ISSN 1321–5698.

Another factor women have felt the need to counter has been the so-called Christian anthropology exemplified in Manfred Hauke's analysis written, as the subtitle puts it, 'in the Light of the Order of Creation and Redemption'. This divinely established order reveals men as constitutionally 'more likely to be suited to communicating the message of God in its objective content' than women, who tend to 'confuse the personal and the factual'.[18] Less a cause of 'offence'[19] to women but not dissimilar in intent are the many reflections of John Paul II on 'the specific diversity and personal originality of man and woman'.[20] Woman's 'personal resources' are 'different' from man's and, being 'specifically hers', they form the basis of 'her "fulfilment" as a person, her dignity and vocation'. It is this difference from the man that makes it impossible for the woman to act 'in persona Christi' during the sacramental ministry of the Eucharist.[21]

Insistent teaching along this line during the papacy of John Paul II[22] has made it difficult to establish a clear place for women in the official ministry of the church, but a closer consideration of the place in the early church of the ministry of the word would seem to lead us out of some of the contemporary impasses. While there can be no doubt that in the third generation of early Christians women were disbarred from ecclesial roles (1 Tim 2:11–12), this is most likely to be understood as having developed at precisely that period. As suggested by Philip Harland, we can associate it with the growing assimilation of certain Greco-Roman cultural values evident in the Pastoral letters, in this instance limiting women to the household.[23] In the Pauline decades, by contrast, ample indications of the intimate collaboration of women in evangelisation reveal a wholly different status of women within the

---

18. *Women in the Priesthood? A systematic Analysis in the Light of the Order of Creation and Redemption*, English translation (San Francisco: Ignatius, 1988), 257.

19. The word is Hauke's own (257 note 285).

20. *Mulieris dignitatem*, English translation (Homebush, NSW: St Paul , 1988), 40 (paragraph 10).

21. *Mulieris dignitatem*, 94 (paragraph 26).

22. For example, *I will give you shepherds*, English translation (Boston: St Paul, 1992), paragraphs 15, 21; Instruction from the Congregation for the Clergy, *The Priest, Pastor and Leader of the Parish Community* (Strathfield, NSW: St Pauls, 2003), paragraphs 2, 8.

23. *Associations, Synagogues and Congregations: Claiming a Place in Ancient Mediterranean Society* (Minneapolis: Fortrress, 2003), 194.

communities.[24] Among the several women whose collaboration Paul acknowledges in Romans 16:1–16, we note Phoebe ('a delegate' to Rome for her church in Cenchreae),[25] Prisca and her husband ('fellow workers in Christ Jesus' with a 'church in their house'), Junia (one among 'apostles'),[26] Tryphaena and Tryphosa ('workers in the Lord'), and Persis (who also 'worked hard in the Lord'); in addition, Euodia and Syntyche, who 'laboured side by side with me in the gospel together with Clement and the rest of my fellow workers' (Phil 4:3). Much has been written of such collaboration, much of it in the light of Paul's proclamation that 'in Christ . . . there is neither male nor female' (Gal 3:28).[27]

Much of the scholarship invested in the roles of early Christian women has been by women, and one significant but contested issue has been the position adopted towards women by Luke the evangelist. Earlier generations of commentators had frequently honoured Luke for

---

24. With many, I read the passage in 1 Corinthians 14:34–35 as a later interpolation. See Gordon Fee, *The First Epistle to the Corinthians* (Grand Rapids: Eerdmans, 1987), 699–708; Brendan Byrne, *Paul and the Christian Woman* (Homebush, NSW: St Paul, 1988), 59–65.

25. *Diakonia*, 224–25; see also my *Deacons and the Church: Making connections between old and new* (Leominster, UK: Gracewing, 2002), 73-76.

26. In a comprehensive demolition of the argument advanced by Michael Burer and Daniel Wallace, 'Was Junia Really an Apostle? A Re-examination of Rom 16:7', *New Testament Studies* 47 (2000): 76–91, Linda Belleville has definitively established on grounds of ancient Greek usage that Paul intended to acknowledge Junia as 'notable among' the apostles and not merely 'well-known *to* the apostles'; see '*Iounian . . . epis_moi en tois apostolois*: A Re-examination of Romans 16:7 in Light of Primary Source Materials', *New Testament Studies* 51 (May 2005): 231–249.

27. Samples are the essays by J Massyngberde Ford, Bernadette Brooten, Adela Yarbro Collins and others in *Women Priests* (above note 3); Elisabeth M Tetlow, *Women and Ministry in the New Testament* (New York: Paulist Press, 1980); Elisabeth Schüssler Fiorenza, *In Memory of Her: A Feminist Theological Reconstruction of Christian Origins* (London: SCM, 1983); Florence M Gillman, *Women Who Knew Paul* (Collegeville: Liturgical Press, 1992); Bonnie Thurston, *Women in the New Testament* (New York: Crossroad, 1998); and essays in *Women and Christian Origins*, ed Ross Shepard Kraemer and Mary Rose D'Angelo (New York: Oxford, 1999).

the prominence he gave to women, particularly in his gospel. However, with the claim that their prominence in the gospel narrative as exemplary disciples was counterbalanced by their silencing as witnesses in the narrative of Acts, his gospel suddenly became 'an extremely dangerous text', portraying women 'as models of subordinate service, excluded from the power centre of the movement and from significant responsibilities'.[28] A leading voice in this critique has been that of Elisabeth Schüssler Fiorenza, and one important part of her argument centres on the claim that Luke has manipulated the early Christian terms for mission and ministry (*diakon-*) to exclude women from roles in mission and restrict them to the household.[29] While I have attempted to show that her argument, which is widely accepted,[30] is fatally flawed on the grounds of her misreading of the *diakon-* words,[31] I feel that we have much to learn from Luke on women's capacity for ministry of the word. In illustration I choose some reflections on the woman healed of the flow of blood (Luke 8:42b–48).

3. 'Who touched me?'

Luke's Galilean ministry of the Messiah, Lord and Saviour opened in the synagogue of Nazareth with promise of great things for the dispossessed (4:16–22) and quickly developed a powerful impetus as people sought out Jesus, who grasped his mission to 'preach the good news of the kingdom of God' (4:42–44). Beginning at 8:4, Luke presents

---

28 Jane Schaberg, 'Luke' in *The Women's Bible Commentary*, edited by Carol A Newsom and Sharon H Ringe (Louisville, KY: West-minster/John Knox Press, 1992), 275.

29. 'The Practice of Interpretation: Luke 10:38–42' in *But She Said: Feminist Practices of Biblical Interpretation* (Boston: Beacon Press, 1992), 52–76.

30. For example, by Barbara E. Reid, *Choosing the Better Part? Women in the Gospel of Luke* (Collegeville: Liturgical Press, 1996), 144–62. Contrast, Turid Karlsen Seim's dissatisfaction with Schüssler Fiorenza's interpretation of Luke 10:38–42 in *The Double Message: Patterns of Gender in Luke-Acts* (Nashville: Abingdon, 1994), 99–100.

31. For my critique of her position and for further bibliography see 'Did Luke intend a disservice to women in the Martha and Mary story?', *Biblical Theology Bulletin* 28/3 (1998): 104–11; 'Does equality of discipleship add up to church? A critique of Feminist *Ekklesia-*logy', *New Theology Review* 12/3 (August 1999): 48–57.

profound reflections on the bounteous character of 'the word of God' (8:11) liberally scattered like seed, on its power, and on what it demands of those who receive it. The word at once places the disciple in an enlightened phase (8:16) during which the disciple must be deeply intent on listening (8:18). This is no ordinary listening but issues at once in commitment to action; his mother and brothers exemplify what this means because in hearing 'the word of God' they 'do it' (8:21). The antithesis of this godly family are the disciples especially chosen to listen deeply to the word, but who are immediately deaf to it once the storm at sea breaks (8:24): 'We are perishing.' In the calm moments following, they know they have no faith: 'Who then is this . . . ?' The two gripping stories that follow—the mad man living alone among the dead and the two females, woman and girl—reveal the impact of the life force in the word of God and what it demands. The mad man, freed of his demons, tried to join Jesus on the return voyage to Galilee, but Jesus told him to return to the home of his childhood—long since never seen—and 'declare how much God has done' for him. And he went 'proclaiming throughout the whole city how much Jesus had done for him.' (8:39). The saving presence of God in Jesus was the word that the chosen disciples could not hear.

Let us turn to the woman. She has no name. She turns up in the story of the girl, daughter of Jairus, 'a ruler of the synagogue', who is sick and soon to die, but she is twelve and thus verging on womanhood. The woman, by contrast, has suffered these same twelve years, losing her womanhood through a grave menstrual disorder. Far from being of the synagogue like the girl, the woman's condition renders her permanently unclean (Lev 15:25–27), rendering unclean all objects and people she is in contact with and excluding her not only from the synagogue but from her family and community. This well-known pathetic creature forces herself through the crowd to reach Jesus, who walks with the ruler of the synagogue. Luke writes that the crowd 'pressed' around him, in Greek a word closely related to the word in the parable of the seed where the thorns 'choked' the new growth. This woman, however, was not going to let the hustling crowd choke off her drive for health and life. She reached through and touched the teacher's garments, 'immediately' knowing the flow had ceased, her life remade, her horizons new.

The teacher also knew, and knew as well what this required of the woman, so he asked, 'Who was it that touched me?' But 'all denied it'. The movement has halted. Peter, the leader, is deaf to the significance of the moment and tries to brush the question aside. But the teacher is demanding a resolution to the situation created by the touching, and the woman was drawn inexorably and 'trembling' to her moment of judgment. She was known to all. Her status in law was known to the leader of the synagogue, in whose presence she had violated the prescription of Leviticus, and before whom and this teacher she now had to admit her guilt. But a sudden inspiration seized her. She would not confess to a violation of law. She would proclaim her faith in Jesus.

Luke is precise about the character of this moment. Where, in his version, Mark states that the woman told Jesus 'the whole truth' (Mark 5:33), Luke crafts a credal formula: 'she came trembling, and falling down before him proclaimed in the presence of all the people the reason why she had touched him and how she had been healed at once' (8:47). Jesus knew very well her 'reason'. She had come to believe he was a saviour. So whereas Jesus had to ask the disciples, 'Where is your faith?' (8:25), to this woman he could say, 'your faith saved you.' And he addressed her as 'daughter' because from that moment of salvation she was no longer an outsider but a healthy, pure member of the family of God. And a woman again. 'Go in peace,' was the last word of the Master because she had demonstrated to Peter how strong faith needs to be, to the leader of the synagogue how much faith he would need if his daughter were likewise to be saved, and to all the people that this was the Messiah, Lord and Saviour.

This woman's confession of faith in the presence of 'all the people'—a faith to which Peter could not rise—anticipates the faith of the other better known women who attended the tomb of Jesus, came to believe him risen, and 'proclaimed' this to the eleven and all the rest. 'But these words seemed to the apostles an idle tale, and they did not believe them' (Luke 24:12).

The cry of Roman Catholic women today for recognition of their competency in ordained ministry has long been characterised at hierarchical levels of their church as 'an idle tale'. Might not reflection on Luke's story suggest that today's cry is a further echo of a brave prophetic woman in Luke's narrative who accepted the challenge from Jesus to proclaim the word of faith—against all convention—in a crowded street? If so, Luke is a friend indeed to Roman Catholic women to have bequeathed us this story for use in these times. Luke was a very ecclesiologically minded writer.

Women and the Ordained Ministry: Theological Considerations from an Orthodox Perspective

Philip Kariatlis
Sydney

1. Introductory remarks

Questions about the place of women in society at large and specifically within the church have given the Christian Churches cause to reflect on the role of women in different ecclesial ministries. Such questions have nearly always led to queries regarding their access to the ordained ministry. In the twentieth century, certain Churches whose roots are found in the sixteenth century Protestant Reformation, including those of the Anglican tradition, decided to ordain women to the priesthood and episcopate. The Orthodox Churches as a whole rejected this initiative, claiming that it clearly marks a break from the apostolic tradition.[1] They have strongly challenged the argument that the ancient practice of ordaining only males was based on merely sociological factors conditioned by the dominant patriarchal society. However, in claiming that the ordination of women is contrary to the apostolic teaching, the Orthodox tradition in no way upholds contempt for women.[2] It has always recognised the dignity of women and

---

1. Disagreement regarding the ordination of women has led to a discouraging rift within the ecumenical movement. Churches that do not ordain women question how two mutually exclusive perspectives can be reconciled. See 'The Ordination of Women: An Ecumenical Problem', *Concerning the Ordination of Women* (Geneva: World Council of Churches, 1964), 5–11.
2. Early church documents, such as the *Apostolic Church Order* [Adolf Harnack, *Sources of Apostolic Canons,* translated by John Owen (London: Norgate, 1895)] reveal that the pre-Nicene Church included both men and women in local ministry. There is evidence of the bishop, presbyter, the reader and deacons, but also the widows and the women deacons. The question today is not so much why women can not become

affirmed their universal place in the economy of salvation. The role model for all women in the Orthodox Church has been Jesus' mother, understood not as a passive woman but as a resolute and creative personality, as is evidenced by her dialogue with the angel at the Annunciation.

In traditionally Orthodox countries, especially where the church was either openly persecuted or merely tolerated, it was women who heroically assumed the responsibility to protect and preserve the faith within their homes. Feminist ideology has remained foreign to women in Eastern Europe and the Middle East.[3] For Orthodox women, the church is not a male bastion to be conquered. Orthodox women continue to be the soul of the church in their love and sacrifice for the faith. The many lists of female saints include some who have even been praised as 'equal to the apostles' in recognition of their ministry to the church.[4]

Orthodox theology is not so much concerned with discovering the truth of the Church's teaching on the ordination of women as with articulating and clarifying the theological presuppositions embedded within its tradition. It takes seriously the historical fact that the Church has never ordained women throughout its two thousand-year history. This historical reality cannot easily be dismissed since the early church faced the question of women's access to the presbyteral ministry during its confrontation with Gnosticism and Montanism, which had female bishops and presbyters.[5]

Admittedly, certain Orthodox theologians, while not openly advocating the ordaining of women, argue that there are no theological reasons for a prohibition. Ware writes:

---

priests but rather, in light of the rich diversity of ministries in the early church, what are the distinctive gifts conferred by God upon women. Cf Kallistos Ware, 'Man, Woman and the Priesthood of Christ', *Women and the Priesthood,* edited by Thomas Hopko (Crestwood, NY: SVS Press, 1999), 12.

3.   Cf Elizabeth Behr-Sigel, 'The Ordination of Women: a Point of Contention in Ecumenical Dialogue', *St Vladimir's Theological Quarterly,* 48:1 (2004): 51.

4.   The church canonised certain women who served as secular rulers. For example, Empress Irene was instrumental in upholding the truth about venerating icons in the eighth century.

5.   The early church decided that the office of such women who wished to be integrated back into the canonical church be not accepted.

In 1978, I considered the ordination of women to be an impossibility. Now I am much more hesitant. I am far from convinced by many of the current arguments advanced in favour of women priests; but at the same time a number of the arguments urged on the other side now appear to me a great deal less conclusive than they did twenty years ago.[6]

At the Fifth World Conference on Faith and Order in Santiago de Compostela (1993), Ware openly expressed his 'private opinion' that the Orthodox Church might ordain women. To this Archbishop Stylianos of Australia, President of the Orthodox delegation representing the Ecumenical Patriarchate, rightly asserted that the role of Orthodox delegates was to convey Orthodox teaching and not private opinion.[7] Hopko noted four other Orthodox scholars who contended that there are no theological reasons prohibiting women from ordained ministry and that, indeed, theology demands their ministry. They were the late Metropolitan Anthony of Sourozh (England), Dr Elizabeth Behr-Sigel (France), Dr Susan Ashbrook Harvey (America) and Dr Constantinos Yokarinis (Greece). Most Orthodox are still opposed to the ordination of women as presbyters and bishops, yet there remains the task of explaining why, and doing this with care and sensitivity in order to contribute positively to the discussion today.

---

6. Kallistos Ware, 'Man, Woman and the Priesthood of Christ', 7.
7. Archbishop Stylianos has often related this incident during his lectures at St Andrew's Greek Orthodox Theological College, Sydney. Another Orthodox leader who had expressed his desire to ordain women was the late Metropolitan Anthony (Bloom) of Sourozh; see Elizabeth Behr-Sigel, 'The Ordination of Women: An Ecumenical Problem', *Sobornost* 13.1 (1991): 35. At a dialogue between the Orthodox Church and the Old Catholic Communities in 1996, Kallis argued, 'We have arrived at the conclusion that there is no theological or dogmatic justification for definitively prohibiting the ordination of women to priestly ministry. A determining consideration was that of the Church's soteriological dimension and vocation: the salvation of mankind and of all creation in Jesus Christ. It is our common human nature in its entirety, man and woman, which our Lord assumed'; cf Urs von Ars and Anastasios Kallis eds, *Bild Christi und Geschlecht, Internationale Kirchliche Zeitschrift*, 88.2 (1988): 22.

2. The three crucial issues connected with women's ordination—an overview

At least three crucial questions are to be considered. Firstly, there is the question whether the past exclusion of women from the ordained ministry simply reflected the cultural and social milieu of the time. Those convinced by such a proposition would argue that the church today should have women bishops/presbyters to reflect the far-reaching changes in the status of women in society and political life today where they are included in almost every facet of public life. Is this argument credible?

Churches whose rites have often changed find it difficult to appreciate why women cannot be introduced to the liturgical priesthood as a sign of engagement with 'modern' times. This attitude may be countered by an appeal to tradition,[8] which safeguards the integrity of the church and its continuity with the apostolic times. Tradition evidences one simple fact: neither Christ himself, nor the church, appointed women to the ordained ministry. Even the Virgin Mary, an icon of human perfection, and one who might be considered most appropriate as a candidate for special ministry in the church, was not given this ordination.[9]

Secondly, the biblical witness to the ordained ministry must be considered. Since the bishop/presbyter is said to share in the priesthood of Christ, Christ's male mode of existence must be given its rightful significance. Maleness is one of the necessary qualifications of the ordained minister that cannot be ignored or set aside if one is to take seriously the biblical standards for ecclesial leadership.

Thirdly, it is clear that the question of the ordination of women is inextricably linked to Christian anthropology. It will be shown that three areas of anthropology, ontology, permanency of gender and the

---

8.   Tradition is not to be understood merely as social customs that the church adopted over the centuries. It is the ongoing presence of the life of the Holy Spirit within the Church. What has been received by generations before is received and handed on integrally and creatively, not mechanically. Hence the great sense of continuity in the Orthodox Church in line with the constancy of Jesus Christ (Heb 3:8).

9.   Many fathers of the church, most notably St Epiphanius of Salamis (d.403), argued along this line. St Ephiphanius stated, 'God never appointed to this ministry a single woman upon earth' (*Panarion* 79,2,3–79,7,4).

hierarchical implications of gender, work together with the church's understanding of the hypostasised nature of God and humanity to render priesthood for women an ontic impossibility.

Finally, an investigation into the above three areas will lead into a theology of the ordained ministry itself and the Orthodox understanding of the iconic character of the priesthood as it images the historical person of Christ. Orthodoxy stresses the significance of Christ's masculine mode of existence for exercising the ordained ministry. Notwithstanding this emphasis, it must be noted that not every form of the ordained ministry, such as the diaconate, is to be denied to women. Nor can it be denied that the progressive clericalisation of the church has taken away other ministries exercised by women in the early church, which must be rediscovered today.

3. Is the exclusion of women to the priesthood merely culturally conditioned?

It is argued that it was only natural that women were prohibited from such a ministry in the past.[10] Yet it would hardly be faithful to history to suggest that the reasons why the church did not ordain women are cultural. Indeed, the early church proclaimed and defended radically counter-cultural teachings and practices repugnant to both Jews and Greeks, which by comparison would make any institution of women bishops and priests insignificant.[11]

For example, Greek philosophy devised cosmological theories inseparably linking eternal divine being with the created world and claiming that matter was pre-existent either through the world of ideas (Plato), the logos (Stoics) or the unmoved mover (Aristotle). The church upheld an ontological gap between the world and God, teaching that the world was created *ex nihilo* and was therefore not preexistent.

---

10. Arguments in favour of women's ordination usually assert that just as it was right for the church to 'innovate' by abolishing slavery, today it must also cease discriminating against women by not allowing them to be ordained. But the Patristic corpus is entirely clear in its opposition to slavery. See St Basil's remark, 'no one is a slave by nature' (*On the Holy Spirit*, 20,51. PG 32:160D).

11. See Thomas Hopko, 'Presbyter/Bishop: A Masculine Ministry', *Women and the Priesthood*, edited by Thomas Hopko (Crestwood, NY: SVS Press, 1999), 140.

Another counter-cultural element was Jesus' use of the term *abba* (daddy)[12] to refer to the transcendent and indescribable God. The name of the deity was not pronounced among the Israelites, and the diminutive form of Father, *abba*, to refer to God would have been appalling to the Jewish mind which understood God as 'impalpable, uncircumscribed, incomprehensible, and unfathomable'[13] and beyond gender. Jesus' use of the term *abba* did reveal that God could be known and named through his Son who revealed God as Father.[14]

The assertion that a male-centred culture devised masculine names for God rejects the revelatory character of the Scriptures and the entire body of the divinely inspired canon (2 Tim 3:16).[15] According to Orthodox doctrine, God who is without gender is nevertheless revealed to the world in gender specific imagery. To reject the scriptural names of God as Father who begets a divine Son and sends forth his Holy Spirit would be to alter radically the divine mystery

---

12. Cf Mark 14:35, also Rom 4:5 and Gal 4:6.

13. St John Damascus, *An Exact Exposition of the Orthodox Faith*, Book 1, chapter 2.

14. The hypostatic characteristic of God as Father was understood specifically in relation to Jesus Christ and the Holy Spirit, and surpassed human notions of father or masculinity in general. St Gregory Nyssa noted: 'It is clear that this metaphor contains a deeper meaning than the obvious one . . . ' (*Against Eunomius*, 1. *NPNF*, vol 5, 63); 'each one of these names [Father, Son and Holy Spirit] has a human sound, but not a human meaning, so also that of Father . . . ' (vol 5, 93).

15. For the Orthodox understanding of divine inspiration see Stylianos Harkianakis, *The Infallibility of the Church in Orthodox Theology* [in Greek] (Athens, 1965), 17–23, and Theodore Stylianopoulos, 'The Nature of Holy Scripture: Divine and Human Aspects', *The New Testament: An Orthodox Perspective* (Brookline, Mass: Holy Cross Press, 1999), 32–43.

16. St Athanasius argued against using such terms for God because they described God's *common activity* towards the world and not 'who' the persons are. Such terms destroy God's absolute freedom in that they make him contingent upon creation. God could only be Creator from the point that the world was created, but God is God before the world comes into existence. See *Contra Arians* 1,33 as explained by Florovsky in *Aspects of Church History, The Collected Works of Georges Florovsky* vol 4 (Belmont, Mass: Norland Publishing Co, 1975), 52f. God is eternally Father because from him the Son was eternally begotten and the Holy Spirit proceeds from the Father eternally.

revealed in the dispensation of salvation. Other names such as Creator, Redeemer and Sanctifier,[16] are not the scriptural hypostatic names but describe the way all three persons of the tri-hypostatic Godhead personally act in a common way towards the world. The Father creates, redeems, sustains and governs the world through his divine Son and in his Holy Spirit·[17]

Clearly, throughout his earthly life Jesus was not bound to the social norms of his time. He ate with tax collectors and sinners (Mark 2:16) and spoke with women of ill repute such as the Samaritan woman near Jacob's well (John 4:7). Famous sayings of Jesus show a striking independence from contemporary customs. In speaking to his disciples about fulfilling the Law, Jesus said, 'You have heard that it was said . . . but I say to you . . .' (Matt 5:21–22). He not only claimed to be 'lord of the Sabbath' (Matt 12:8) but that the Sabbath was made for humankind and not humankind for the Sabbath (Mark 2:27).

Finally, the church which is said to be 'the pillar and bulwark of the truth' (1Tim 3:15) that is infallible,[18] could not err on such a foundational issue as to who would be appointed to continue officially Christ's ministry on earth. Christ promised to send the Holy Spirit to guide the church into all truth (John 16:13). If then it can be accepted that it was not past cultural conditions that excluded women from the priesthood,[19] it must be asserted that present practice in the Church cannot be based on changes in society. As we shall see from the biblical witness, an innovation would bring about a rupture from the apostolic faith (see Heb 7:12).

---

17. Distinguishing between the hypostatic names and the names used to describe God's activity in the world is important. Confusion can lead to a distortion in the trinitarian mystery. Metaphorical names in Scripture to describe God, such as rock, morning star, a mother, cannot be used to address God.

18. For the infallibility of the Church from an Orthodox perspective, see Stylianos Harkianakis, *The Infallibility of the Church in Orthodox Theology* [in Greek], (Athens, 1965).

19. That women were not seen as inferior to men is clear from the Synaxarion (Lives of Saints) of the Church; there are canonised women saints in every category. They include apostle, prophet, martyr, ascetic, monastic, missionary, evangeliser, healer, holy physician, helper to the poor, fools for Christ, but not presbyter or bishop. Sanctity is possible for all human beings irrespective of gender.

4. Biblical witness to the ordained ministry

That the ancient practice of ordaining certain men to the priesthood did not reflect an arbitrary practice influenced by contemporary patriarchal culture does not theologically explain why women have not been admitted to the ordained ministry. Orthodox theology understands the bishop/presbyter as the sacrament of Christ's headship and presence, so a brief discussion of the theological significance of Christ's maleness as distinct from his humanity is needed.

In the New Testament, the church is portrayed as a theanthropic institution, comprised of a community of believers intimately united to Christ (the head of the church) and to one another, thus forming the one body of the Lord. Because of its communal nature, the church throughout the centuries has claimed to be the sacramental and spiritual presence of Christ on earth.[20] According to the New Testament, in continuing the work of the apostles, the bishop/presbyter[21] actualised the sacramental presence of, and unity in, Christ. [22] While the apostles, who had witnessed the resurrection, continued the ministry of Jesus with their preaching, thereby ensuring continuity in the faith, the significant moment for the development of the ordained ministry came when the first witnesses died.[23] The early church had to find a way to perpetuate the integrity and presence of the Lord's teaching as attested by the apostles. The ordained ministry came to be seen as that special grace bestowed on some who would be empowered to build up of the body of Christ in the unity of the faith so that, filled with the Holy Spirit, it could be assured of the presence of the risen Lord. Thus St Ignatius of Antioch could say that the bishop

---

20.   Cf 1Cor 10:16–17; Eph 1:22–23 and Col 1:18.

21.   In Acts and the Pastoral Letters *episkopos* and *presbyteros* are used interchangeably; only after the apostolic era were these titles differentiated. Osborne claims that what the term *presbyteros* meant for the Jewish Christian community, *episkopos* meant for the non Jewish Christian groups; see Kenan B Osborne, *Priesthood: A History of the Ordained Ministry in the Roman Catholic Church* (New York NY: Paulist Press, 1988), 51.

22.   The office of the bishop/presbyter developed within the context of a theology of the church and its apostolic character. Therefore it is never a right of any individual.

23.   For the eschatological significance of the Twelve and their difference to the ministry of the bishop see Stylianos Harkianakis, *The Infallibility of the Church in Orthodox Theology* [in Greek], (Athens, 1965), 39–49.

re-presented (made present) Christ here on earth in the 'type' and 'place' of Christ.[24] From New Testament times, the church has always known an official male ministry which it esteemed 'very highly in love' since it was God himself who had appointed 'first apostles, second prophets, third teachers' (1 Cor 12:28), also 'bishops and deacons' (Phil 1:1).

Based on the New Testament view of the ordained ministry, the early church developed a rich vocabulary for official ministry, going beyond the purely sacerdotal categories, which came to prevail especially in the West during the Middle Ages. Far from being understood in narrowly sacral terms, the priest[25] was also the leader, the president of a community, a teacher, one who officiated in sacral acts, a healer of souls and an initiator of mysteries. Whatever title was used, the bishop/presbyter was understood to be a sacramental or iconic presence of Christ in the community of the faithful.[26] Fighting against

---

24. See Archbishop Stylianos, 'The Most Dangerous "Deus Ex Machina"', *Vema* Nov (2003): 4/26.

25. Some traditions have argued that Christ's priesthood, especially as it is described in the Letter to the Hebrews, has made all other forms of priesthood obsolete. Christians as a whole are called 'priests' (1Pet 2:9). The term 'priest' came to be used to describe the ordained ministry by the late second century AD after Christianity's separation from Judaism. This coincided with the church's interpretation of the eucharist as the sacrificial offering of Jesus Christ (made by the faithful in and through Christ), an offering of thanksgiving to God for saving the world. Jesus was the perfect 'once for all' sacrifice for the sins of the entire world (Heb 7:27). Nevertheless the ministerial priesthood is believed to be a new priesthood founded by Christ. Those called 'priests' sacramentally make present the one perfect sacrifice of Christ as he perpetually offers himself to the Father on behalf of the world. The term *iereus* came to be used to describe the minister's function as president over the eucharist (*episkopos*) and as an elder (*presbyteros*) appointed to direct and administer the community. It echoed the biblical priesthood texts found in Exod 19:6; Isa 61:6 1Pt 2:9 and Rev 1:6; 5:10 and 20:6. The importance of the sacral model of the priesthood is emphasised throughout the patristic literature. Chrysostom devoted two of his six books on the *Priesthood* to this subject.

26. This implies that it be carried out in communion with, and service towards, others. St Gregory of Nyssa states that the priest receives the grace of the Holy Spirit 'as part of' the eucharistic assembly and never apart from the priest's ministry; any vocation could only be realised

iconoclasm in the ninth century, St Theodore the Studite had the following to say regarding priesthood:

> Standing between God and humanity, the priest in the priestly invocations is an imitation of Christ. For the apostle says: 'There is one God, and one mediator between God and people, the man Jesus Christ' (1Tim 2:5). Thus the priest is an icon of Christ.[27]

According to Theodore the priesthood did not belong to the ordained minister since he was not 'another' priest alongside Christ, nor did he offer a sacrifice different from Christ's own loving sacrifice as priest *par excellence*. Rather, just as icons made present the archetype represented, so too the ordained minister existed for no other reason than to make Christ sacramentally present to the community.[28] Such an understanding of the priesthood highlights its male character if it is to image Christ, the God-man, faithfully.[29]

The Pastoral Letters (1Tim 3:1–7; Tit 1:5–9) list various personal qualities an ordained minister was expected to possess. They are all qualities of Christ himself, which confirms that Christ was seen as the source of all ordained ministry. Christ's ministry was complete and could not be added to,[30] but the church claimed to share in this mission and to be an extension of it.[31] All ministry, including that of the ordained priesthood, was seen to be derived from Jesus' all sufficient redemptive ministry. The fundamental biblical viewpoint

---

within the community and never in isolation (PG 46:581D–584A). Thus the specific vocation of certain male persons to the ordained ministry is not an individually possessed power (*potestas*); it has an ecclesial or communal character.

27. *Seven Chapters against the Iconoclasts*, 4. PG 99:493C.

28. Through the words, the paint and the wood, icons too make present the invisible and intangible realities of the kingdom and are therefore often referred to as 'windows to eternity'.

29. See below for the iconic nature of the ordained ministry.

30. In this regard Küng wrote, 'Jesus Christ . . . is himself *the* apostle, prophet, teacher, evangelist, pastor and deacon'; Hans Küng, *The Church* (London: Burn & Oates, 1968), 395.

31. The resurrected Christ commissioned the apostles to continue in his ministry, promising to send the Spirit to equip them for their task. (Matt 28:18–20; Mark 16:15f; Luke 24:46–49 and John 20:21–23).

holds that all those who taught, edified the people of God or administered the sacraments, did so after the pattern of Jesus' priestly ministry and continued his messianic mission. While the emergence of the threefold office of bishop/presbyter/deacon was a gradual development, it came to be established in the church as a way to give Jesus' charisms permanence. In the attempt to provide guidelines for this fixed and defined form of ministry, the New Testament Scriptures provided some guidelines for the church's good order, effective service and witness to the world.[32]

The gender specific nature of the ordained ministry is implicit in the Pastoral Epistles. First Timothy spells out what is entailed in such a leadership role by listing fourteen qualities for effective ministry. The author[33] begins by stressing the nobility of such a ministry and the requirement that leaders be above reproach (1Tim 3:1-2).[34] The bishop who is God's steward here on earth has to be 'above reproach' (1Tim 3:3), 'blameless' (1Tim 1:6), 'the husband of one wife' (1Tim 3:2), clear-minded, meek, slow to anger, not addicted to alcohol, not violent or greedy. He has to be hospitable, gentle, a lover of goodness, prudent, upright, devout and self-controlled. Timothy also states the importance of the bishop managing his household well and being a respected member of the community. Clearly, the requirement that a bishop/presbyter be 'the husband of one wife' would suggest the male character of the ordained ministry. In carrying out their ministry, the bishops or presbyters were considered 'fathers' of the community where God alone was Father. And as 'father' and leader of the

---

32. By the end of the first century there is evidence of three distinct offices in the church. St Ignatius of Antioch envisioned a local church headed by one bishop and consisting of the presbytery and the diaconate (*Philadelphians* 4:1) where all were harmoniously united as strings are to a harp (*Ephesians* 4:1).

33. Saints Ignatius of Antioch, Polycarp and Clement of Alexandria are some of the early church fathers who attribute the letters of Timothy to the apostle Paul.

34. St Silouan of Mount Athos (d. 1938) wrote concerning the nobility of the priesthood, 'This grace is so exceedingly great that were men able to see the glory of this grace, the whole world would wonder at it; but the Lord has veiled it that his servants should not be puffed up but find salvation in humility . . . Truly noble is a priest—the minister of God's altar' (cited in Sophrony Sakharov, *St Silouan the Athonite* (Crestwood, NY: SVS Press, 1999), 400-4.

community, the ordained minister safeguarded and preserved the church's visible unity, continuity and identity with Christ. As 'father' of a local community the ordained minister had to be a man.

The responsibilities implied in such leadership serve to indicate the limitations on women's ministry in this regard. Just as leadership in the family or the household was placed with the husband,[35] so also leadership in the church was understood to be given from above to those who were head of their household. First Timothy makes this connection clearly: 'He must manage his own household well, keeping his children submissive and respectful in every way—for if someone does not know how to manage his own household, how can he take care of God's church?' (1Tim 3:4–5).

It was in exercising his ministry as leader, head,[36] king,[37] bridegroom,[38] son[39] and husband to his bride, the church, that the maleness of the ordained minister was understood to be one of the many prerequisites. Women were not expected to fulfil such roles within the community.

5. Anthropological argument

Christian anthropology highlights that ordained ministry is an ontic impossibility for women. It consolidates the biblical witness to the male character of the Christian priesthood. With respect to the ontology of gender, two schools of thought have emerged within Orthodox theology. Both would affirm the equality of men and women. The specific disagreement is whether this distinction is a creaturely limitation brought about by the Fall and so must be overcome, or whether the sexual complementarity is a permanent part of God's creative will and given for the enrichment and fulfilment of life.[40] Which view is espoused will determine not only any meaningful sense of gender but also one's theology of the ordained ministry. Failure to appreciate the importance of gender distinction in the divine plan for humanity's salvation can lead to the justification of women's

---

35. 1Cor 11:3; Eph 5:21–23; Col 3:18.
36. Eph 5:23.
37. Luke 19:38.
38. Matt 9: 14–5.
39. John 1:18.
40. It is difficult to see how the former belief can be reconciled with Christ recalling that God made humans as male and female (Matt 19:4).

ordination if there is nothing in female human nature to render ordained ministry impossible for her.

Those who downplay the importance of sexual differentiation believe it to be a post-lapsarian biological phenomenon with no enduring importance for God's vision of creation. Gender is one the 'garments of skins' brought about by the Fall. It relates merely to one's 'biological hypostasis' which must be transcended in Christ's new covenant. To this school, most notably amongst the Orthodox, belong Karras,[41] Harrison,[42] Behr-Sigel[43] and Yokarinis.[44] However, rejecting the importance of sexual distinction can lead to the belief that there is no hindrance to women being admitted to the priesthood since its archetype is Christ's genderless humanity. Convinced that sexuality is temporary and must ultimately be transcended, Harrison and Yokarinis are led to this conclusion. Harrison remarks that anthropological arguments

> involve serious theological problems . . . For the Greek
> fathers, gender is clearly absent in the divine nature . . .
> The defining concept in patristic anthropology is the
> image of God in humanity, which entails an intrinsic
> link and correlation between the human and the
> divine. To be human is first and above all to live by

---

41. Valerie A Karras, 'Patristic Views on the Ontology of Gender', JT Chirban ed, *Personhood: Orthodox Christianity and the Connection between Body, Mind and Soul* (Westport, CT, and London: Bergin and Garvey, 1996), 113-19.

42. Nonna Verna Harrison, 'Male and Female in Cappadocian Theology', *Journal of Theological Studies* 41:2 (1990): 441-71.

43. 'The male-female duality has no part in the divine image. Sexuality represents a sort of fall into the animal realm, a fall that precedes the fall into sin. It therefore seems like an overprint on the purely spiritual, divine image and does not seem to be penetrated by its radiance'; Elizabeth Behr-Sigel, *The Ministry of Women in the Church,* translated by Steven Bigham (Redondo Beach: California: Oakwood Publications, 1991), 87.

44. Constantinos N Yokarinis, *The Priesthood of Women in the Context of the Ecumenical Movement* [in Greek] (Katerini: Epektasis, 1995). A summary of his thoughts in English can be found in his article 'The Priesthood of Women: Looking at Patristic Teaching', *Orthodox Women Speak: Discerning the 'Signs of the Times'* (Geneva: WCC Publications, 1999), 167-76.

participation in God. It follows that since gender is
absent in the divine Archetype, it is absent in the
human image as well. This means it is not central to
being human . . . gender is a secondary and temporary
feature of the human condition and will no longer be
present in the resurrection body.[45]

Though Harrison argues against women's ordination on the basis
of her iconic understanding of the priesthood in relation to Christ, she
sees no grounds for exclusion based on gender considerations. She is
correct in stating that there is no gender in the Godhead but in arguing
that a person is neither intrinsically male nor female, she takes away
the mode by which all human persons are *en-fleshed* and exist in
history. It may be conceptually possible to speak of human nature as
an idea without taking into account its gender-specific *hypostasis* (ie a
unique existence of nature), but it remains outside the parameters of
reality.[46] Three basic convictions of Christian anthropology will serve
to refute objections to the permanency of gender and, by extension,
claims in favour of the female priesthood.

---

45. Nonna Verna Harrison, 'Orthodox Arguments Against the Ordination of
     Women', *Women and the Priesthood,* edited by Thomas Hopko
     (Crestwood, NY: SVS Press, 1999), 170-74. Yokarinis argues that the
     first Adam was androgynous and separated into male and female by God
     in view of the Fall. Sexuality was not an essential part of human nature.
     In the incarnation, Christ took on the free-fallen state of humanity
     thereby recapitulating the masculine and feminine aspects together
     again. See Constantinos N Yokarinis, *The Priesthood of Women in the
     Context of the Ecumenical Movement* [in Greek] (Katerini: Epektasis,
     1995). Ware also states that 'the anthropological argument, then, at any
     rate in the form in which it has so far been expressed, fails to settle the
     question whether or not women can become ministerial priests' ('Man,
     Woman and the Priesthood of Christ', 39).
46. This argument that the Patristic tradition describes the human person as a
     reality which is above and beyond the categories of masculine, usually
     refers to passages of St Gregory of Nyssa and St Maximus the
     Confessor. It ignores that these statements were written without an
     underlying aim to offer definitive answers on gender. It also ignores the
     consensus Patrum on this issue.

Created in God's image and likeness: male and female

While all men and women are inherently equal in God's sight there are clearly distinct and complementary roles in society, the family and in the church.[47] Sexuality and sexual differentiation, far from being introduced by God in view of the Fall, were part of God's original plan of creation that was 'very good'[48] (Gen 1:28). They are an essential element for humans to be able to reflect and participate in God's trinitarian life whose content is love. The Eastern Christian tradition claims that human beings were created in God's image and according to his likeness *as male and female* from the beginning, and not in view of the Fall (Gen 1.27). Gender distinction and sexuality contribute to human persons being created in the image and according to the likeness of God. Far from being a culturally learned interplay, the masculine/feminine complementarity involves two different and concrete modes of 'being' without which God's creative act would be incomplete. Genesis clearly states that gender and sexuality do not belong only to fallen human nature; gender differentiation is an essential element of what it means to be a human person. Christ confirmed this in speaking about marriage: 'Have you not read that the one who made them *at the beginning* "made them male and female"?' (Matt 19:4). The argument that would downplay or even discard the importance of gender in favour of a common, abstract and genderless human nature cannot stand.[49]

---

47.   Most notable among those who support the equality yet distinctiveness of genders are Paul Evdokimov, *The Sacrament of Love* (Crestwood, NY: SVS Press, 1985); Thomas Hopko, 'God and Gender: Articulating the Orthodox View', *St Vladimir's Theological Quarterly* 37:2&3 (1993): 141–83; Kenneth P Wesche, 'Man and Woman in Orthodox Tradition: The Mystery of Gender, *St Vladimir's Theological Quarterly* 37:2&3 (1993): 213–51; Deborah M Belonick, 'Testing the Spirits', *Women and the Priesthood,* edited by Thomas Hopko (Crestwood, NY: SVS Press, 1999), 189–223.

48.   God fashioned woman from the side of Adam, which means that human persons *together* as man and women constitute the image of God. That God fashioned the woman from the very same substance of the man the Holy Fathers interpreted as a sign of the equality of man and woman. Man cannot alone be in God's image without the woman, neither can woman without man be said to be in the image of God.

49.   The Orthodox tradition emphasises that gender is part of God's original plan because human beings are created in the image of God who is essentially love. The statement 'God is love' (1John 4:8) refers to the

Towards a theology of hypostasis and the ontology of gender

The 'hypostatic' or foundational 'existential' principle consolidates the contention that gender constitutes an inalienable reality at the very core of human beings. The introduction of person—in which gender is obviously included—as an ontological category affirms the personal mode of existence as causative of ontology and not derivative. Just as the divine nature of God does not exist in abstraction but concretely in the persons of Father, Son and Holy Spirit, so too by way of analogy the one nature of humanity, which all persons share, exists specifically either in a 'male' or 'female' mode. Leontius of Jerusalem (sixth century) wrote: 'There is no nature of man that can be observed by itself, but each nature belongs to a particular someone, and is seen as an *enhypostasised* nature.'[50] Gender, far from being a temporary difference that will be transcended in the heavenly realm, acquires an ontological significance since personhood without its particular mode of existence is an ontic impossibility.

Furthermore, according to the Patristic tradition the human hypostasis is a dual unity of soul and body where one element does not overshadow the other or is in opposition to the other.[51] St Irenaeus

---

divine essence itself, which the human person is to emulate in a creaturely way in order to actualise the life of the Holy Trinity. Adam alone without Eve could not image God since he could not love. There must be a communion of love in order to reflect God. But in order to love one must have another person of the same kind yet different to love. 'Gender-differentiation for human beings is an essential element in their ability to reflect and participate in God's divine being and life whose content is love . . . And it is exactly as men and women, and in their intercommunion together, that human beings find and fulfil themselves as creatures made in the image and likeness'; Thomas Hopko, 'God and Gender: Articulating the Orthodox View', *St Vladimir's Theological Quarterly* 37:1&2 (1993): 160. Just as God is not alone in his divinity from all eternity, so too human persons must not be alone but in communion with 'other' persons in order to be what God made them to be: loving creatures. In imaging God, human beings are created to be 'lovers' and this cannot be done without the gender distinction.

50. *Adversus Nestorianos* V,28. PG 86.1, col 1748D.

51. Christos Androutsos rightly notes that 'the right doctrine of the human person protests on the one hand against Materialism . . . and against the over-emphasised stress of certain spiritualising theories which maintain that the body is a kind of mere representation and prison of the soul. . .

of Lyons was clear on this: 'The complete person consists in the commingling and union of the soul that receives the spirit [or breath] of the Father, together with the flesh [or physical nature] that is fashioned according to the image.'[52] The human person is a psychosomatic unity with interdependence of soul[53] and body. This doctrine of personhood is related to gender in so far as it affirms the permanency of the somatic aspect of human nature through which the human person is seen either as male or female. This doctrine receives confirmation by St Paul who did not refer to the dissociation of body and soul after death but to a transfigured body (2 Cor 5:1–3). Paul insisted that the soul will not be 'naked', that is, disincarnate but united with a body, albeit a glorified body, thereby inferring the permanency of gender by way of a transfigured bodily resurrection as men and women. Similarly, Hopko concludes:

> We do not know exactly what we shall be in the new age of God's kingdom . . . but what we do know is that even then human beings will be women and men, not angels or androgynes, and that our gender distinction will remain an essential element in the unending life which God gives us in Christ with possibilities for communion in love which we can now neither conceive nor imagine.[54]

The body does not overshadow the soul, nor imprison the spirit'; *Dogmatics* (Astir: Athens, 1992), 130.

52. *Against the Heresies,* V, vi, 1.
53. The doctrine of the pre-existence of the soul was condemned in the Fifth Ecumenical Council. The view known as Traducianism held that the soul came into existence with the body independent of God, that is, directly through the parents. The theory of Creationism taught that God generated the soul independent of the parents. The danger of this theory was that it could lead to determinism thereby implicating God in the evil of the world. The Scriptures attest God's direct intervention in the creation of the soul (cf Ps 32:15; Zech 12:1; 2 Macc 7:22). Androutsos rightly argues that the right view is a 'combination of the theories of creationism and traducianism, so that the human person would be a result of both divine and human activity' (Androutos, *Dogmatics,* 136).
54. Thomas Hopko, 'God and Gender: Articulating the Orthodox View', *St Vladimir's Theological Quarterly* 37, 1&2 (1993): 182.

The permanency of gender is exemplified in Christ's resurrection. The ten different appearances of Jesus recorded in the New Testament give the impression that Christ appeared visibly and physically, though in a body transformed and liberated from physical limitations. His resurrected body was 'transfigured' and rendered 'spiritual'. Applying this principle on a human level, Belonick rightly states, 'We will not transcend gender and sexuality; our gender and our sexuality will be transfigured'.[55]

A denial or de-emphasis of gender lends support to the ordination of women in that it plays down the significance of Christ's somatic existence on earth as a male, after which the ordained ministry is patterned. The body of Christ is not to be seen simply as a temporary medium best suited for the spreading of the gospel during his time on earth. The Orthodox tradition, based on the Scriptural witness to Christ, underscores also the male mode of his humanity. It believes this is in line with other biblical depictions of Christ as Bridegroom, Head, King, and Son.

Gender and Hierarchy

Connected to the question of the relationship between the tri-hypostatic Godhead and human persons (including their gender) is the issue of order (*taxis*) within the interpersonal life of the Godhead. This has ramifications also for the priesthood. Human communities must reflect the Trinity as a communion between three persons of the Godhead since they are the archetype for the world's communal mode of existence. The Eastern Orthodox fathers spoke of the Father as the 'cause' and 'source' within the life of the tri-hypostatic Godhead,[56] which provides the perfect communion and unity between the three persons. They also referred to the Father as the source of the Son's generation and the Holy Spirit's procession. This conviction was based on their interpretation of the words of Jesus that 'the Father is greater than I' (John 14:28), interpreted as a reference to the Father's un-originate hypostatic quality rather than to the divine essence. The Father was understood to be greater not because his essence was superior but because he was the sole principle of the Godhead. In this

---

55. Deborah M. Belonick, 'Testing the Spirits', *Women and the Priesthood*, edited by Thomas Hopko (Crestwood, NY: SVS Press, 1999), 205.

56. Since there is no notion of time before the creation of the world one cannot speak of the Father, as cause of the Godhead, ever existing without the Son or the Spirit.

case Fatherhood does not imply an ontological superiority over the Son and Spirit, even though they are obedient to the will of the Father. The Son and the Holy Spirit are in no way diminished, because they are consubstantial with the Father and are the Father's eternal glory. Within the Trinity hierarchy and equality are not mutually exclusive categories.

Hopko explains this hierarchical communion, which preserves the equality between Father, Son and Holy Spirit and acts as the model for human communities, in the following way:

> Among human beings, as in nature, there is a communal order which is clearly hierarchical, patterning the hierarchy of the Trinity. When it is what it should be, it is a communion of being and life whose content is love among equals who share an identical nature uniquely 'enhypostasized' in personally distinct 'modes of existence' in imitation of Divinity.[57]

Far from implying power and tyrannical dominance over women on the part of men or an inherent inferiority of women in relation to men, the hierarchical equality posited in the man-woman relationship in the Scriptures carries with it the sense of 'source'. The ontic foundation of men and women[58] is none other than God, affirming the intimate communion and equality between man and woman. Nevertheless there is an ontological priority in man since Adam precedes Eve. Though equal, woman is derived from Adam: 'Indeed, man was not made from woman, but woman from man. Neither was man created for the sake of woman, but woman for the sake of man . . . Nevertheless, in the Lord woman is not independent of man or man independent of woman' (1Cor 11:8–11).

This passage stresses the intimate and loving communion between man and woman, where man's priority or headship is understood in terms of initiating this communion by being the first to love and by

---

57. Thomas Hopko, 'God and Gender: Articulating the Orthodox View', 166,67.

58. The view that Christ is the prototype for men and the Holy Spirit for women runs the risk of dividing the common ontic source of men and women—Christ—and therefore their intimate communion; see Kenneth P Wesche, 'Man and Woman in Orthodox Tradition: The Mystery of Gender', 223.

submitting himself to and serving the woman. Though it may sound rather nonsensical in today's society, Hopko captures the Christian vision in the following way: 'When man submits himself to woman, and gives to her lovingly and freely without asking anything in return, in order to be one with her in every way, then he is truly man'.[59] Without denying the equality of their common humanity, men and women have unique and specific vocations. It is only by observing their equal yet complementary roles that men and women are able by God's grace to transcend gender while remaining 'male' and 'female'.

Relating this to ordination, if the archetype of the ordained ministry is Christ and his ministry as prophet, priest and pastor, then Christ's male mode of existence becomes significant for this unique vocation. The ordained minister is to reflect Christ's ministry as head, leader, bridegroom and husband to his bride, the church. The specific vocation of the ordained minister to sacramentally actualise this within the ecclesial community can only be fulfilled by certain men since women can not be expected to be husband, father or bridegroom of a community. The specificity and distinction of charisms of men and women in Christian anthropology bring to light the importance of Christ's male mode of human existence as an archetypal profile for the ordained ministry.

6. The bishop/presbyter as an 'icon' of Christ

The church claims to share in the very life of the Triune God. Since Christ's sacramental presence is actualised through the church's leadership, the bishop/presbyter is said to be an 'icon' pointing to its archetype: to Christ and his self-emptying love for the church. The Eastern Orthodox tradition claims that since the bishop/presbyter iconically presents Christ to the body of the faithful he must be male in order to do reflect Christ's likeness faithfully. Without further explanation, the argument that 'the ordained priesthood is a male one, because it represents the witness and the sacrifice of the incarnate Christ'[60] would seem unconvincing to some, if not offensive. One

---

59.   Thomas Hopko, 'God and Gender: Articulating the Orthodox View', 168.

60.   Metropolitan Chrysostom of Myra, cited in Gennadios Limouris ed, *The Place of the Woman in the Orthodox Church and the Question of the Ordination of Women* (Katerini: Tertios Publications, 1992), 129–30.

might easily argue that, since both men and women bear the image of God, surely all qualify for ordination. In such arguments Christ's humanity assumes significance but his male gender, if not totally ignored and discarded, is played down as unimportant. This school of thought would place Christ's male gender on equal par, for example, with the colour of his eyes, going so far as to reject outright his 'male' bodily form after the resurrection. Barnhouse argues, 'It was necessary to pick a particular sex in which to incarnate . . . Jesus in the first century had to be and therefore was male, even though the living Christ was androgynous'.[61]

Those who assert that the maleness of Christ is inconsequential maintain that, while Christ was biologically male, psychologically he did not fit into any masculine role but was possessed by both masculine and feminine qualities. However the very fact that Christ was fully human implies that he had a human body and a human soul that existed in male form. It is not the emphasis on Christ's humanity that is rejected by the Orthodox tradition but an emphasis at the expense of his masculinity.

Thus, the Eastern Orthodox understanding of the ordained ministry underscores the ordained person's male 'mode of existence' so as to be an effective sign making present sacramentally Christ who was head, husband, and bridegroom of the community. The presbyter/bishop is *alter Christus* not because he takes the place of Christ but because through him Christ is truly present in the church. St John Chrysostom wrote, 'It is the Father, the Son and the Holy Spirit who perform everything, but the priest lends his tongue and supplies His hand.'[62] In standing before the faithful, the bishop/presbyter makes Christ, the true celebrant, present. And in making Christ present he is also called 'father' in so far as he is the sacramental presence of Christ who makes the Father known in the Spirit, thus making possible an encounter with Christ himself.

---

61.   Ruth Tiffany Barnhouse, 'An Examination of the Ordination of Women to the Priesthood in Terms of the Symbolism of the Eucharist', *Women and Orders*, edited by Robert J Heyer (New York NY: Paulist Press, 1974), 23.

62.   *On the Treachery of Judas* 1,6 (PG 49:380), cited in Kallistos Ware, 'Man, Woman and the Priesthood of Christ', 46.

7. Concluding remarks

In the Orthodox Church's view, all persons—both clergy and laity—who have received the sacraments of baptism and chrismation constitute the body of Christ with the calling to partake in the three-fold ministry of our Lord as king, priest and prophet. Far from being passive members, the entire body of the faithful, both men and women in communion with one another are together called to make Christ present in the world and to contribute towards this sacred task in their own unique way. All human persons created in the image and likeness of God are a 'royal priesthood' and thereby endowed with the potential to bridge the existential gap between the uncreated God and the created world.[63] Human persons were created to reconcile and unite in their person the created world with God and thus enable it to live eternally. For this reason we illustrated the importance of harmony and communion within the community of human persons. Just as in God the real differences between Father, Son and Holy Spirit do not destroy but actualise the perfection of the divinity, so too, analogically speaking, gender difference of human beings does not destroy unity but enhances human life. All men and women are to discover their unique calling as created in the image and according to the likeness of God in order to fulfil this priestly task.

However, given the testimony from tradition, the Orthodox interpretation of Christian anthropology, Christology and the sacramental orders shows that within the royal priestly vocation there is also the specific office of the bishop/presbyter whose ministry bears witness to the presence of Christ's priesthood to the entire community. The iconic understanding of the ordained ministry claims that the bishop/presbyter today sacramentally actualises the presence of Christ himself within the believing community. The anthropological argument affirms the equality of both genders but argues that headship and husbandhood, which define the functional role of the ordained minister, are impossible for the female gender. The maleness of the priest, acting as an iconic symbol in this unique way, forms one qualification amongst others seen to be necessary if the real person of Jesus, including his male mode of existence, is to be imaged so as not to deny any aspect of his incarnation.

---

63.   Cf Christos Yannaras, *The Freedom of Morality* (Crestwood, NY: SVS Press, 1984), 98.

Contributors

Josephine Armour OP is Deputy Principal at St Dominic's Priory College, North Adelaide. In 2000 she completed a thesis on the revision of the theology underpinning the ordained ministry in the Roman Catholic Church.

Peter Bolt is Head of New Testament studies at Moore Theological College, Sydney.

John Collins has written extensively on the origins of Christian ministry and its implications for ministry tody. He teaches a course on ministry at Yarra Theological Union within the Melbourne College of Divinity.

Philip Kariatlis is Academic Secretary at St Andrew's Greek Orthodox Theological College and assistant lecturer in theology to Archbishop Stylianos.

John Kleinig is head of the biblical department at Australian Lutheran College, North Adelaide, specialising in Old Testament, worship, spirituality, and preaching.

Peter Lockwood lectures at Australian Lutheran College, North Adelaide, specialising in Old Testament and theology. He also edits the *Lutheran Theological Journal*.

Vic Pfitzner is a retired former lecturer and principal of Luther Seminary (now Australian Lutheran College), North Adelaide.

Muriel Porter, a Melbourne laywoman, historian and author, has been an advocate of the ordination of women in the Anglican Church for the past twenty years. She was a representative of the Diocese of Melbourne at the 2004 General Synod.

Julia Pitman is Programs Manager at the Australian Centre for Christianity and Culture, at the Canberra Campus of Charles Sturt University.

Stephen Spence is Principal of Burleigh College, Adelaide, which serves the South Australian Baptist Union. His special area of interest is the New Testament.

Geoff Thompson lectures in theology at the Uniting Church's Trinity Theological College, Brisbane, and within the program of the Brisbane College of Divinity.

Cathy Thomson is parish priest at Payneham, South Australia and archdeacon within the Anglican Diocese of Adelaide.

Philip Wilson is the Roman Catholic Archbishop of Adelaide with expertise in canon law.

Next Issue

March 2006

Media and Truth

edited by

Morag Fraser

and

Stephen Crittenden